Back-to-Basics

Parenting in a Chaotic World

Margaret Huber Hackworthy

Back To Basics...Parenting in a Chaotic World © Copyright <<2022>> Margaret Huber Hackworthy

All rights reserved. No part of this publication may be reproduced, distributed or transmitted in any form or by any means, including photocopying, recording, or other electronic or mechanical methods, without the prior written permission of the publisher, except in the case of brief quotations embodied in critical reviews and certain other noncommercial uses permitted by copyright law.

Although the author and publisher have made every effort to ensure that the information in this book was correct at press time, the author and publisher do not assume and hereby disclaim any liability to any party for any loss, damage, or disruption caused by errors or omissions, whether such errors or omissions result from negligence, accident, or any other cause.

Adherence to all applicable laws and regulations, including international, federal, state and local governing professional licensing, business practices, advertising, and all other aspects of doing business in the US, Canada or any other jurisdiction is the sole responsibility of the reader and consumer.

Neither the author nor the publisher assumes any responsibility or liability whatsoever on behalf of the consumer or reader of this material. Any perceived slight of any individual or organization is purely unintentional.

The resources in this book are provided for informational purposes only and should not be used to replace the specialized training and professional judgment of a health care or mental health care professional.

Neither the author nor the publisher can be held responsible for the use of the information provided within this book. Please always consult a trained professional before making any decision regarding treatment of yourself or others.

For more information, email backtobasicsparenting1@gmail.com.

ISBN: 979-8-9859670-0-5 (print only)

ISBN: 979-8-9859670-1-2 (ebook only)

Get your FREE Template!

To get the best experience with this book, I've found readers, who download and use my free template -- Note, Reflect & Take Action, are better able to implement and take the next steps needed to create an action plan that best fits their family's needs or classroom's dynamics.

Note, Reflect & Take Action Template

You can get a copy by visiting one of the following:

backtobasicsparenting1@gmail.com

tinyurl.com/3kdehzpvbtbparentingworld

To my parents and grandparents—for providing a positive environment for us to grow up in while teaching that hard work, sacrifice, perseverance, honesty, grit, and grace create a wonderful life.

Behind you, all your memories.
Before you, all your dreams.
Around you, all who love you.
Within you, all you need.

—Unknown

Contents

Introduction	IX
Lesson #1 Be Present: You Never Get This Time Back	1
Lesson #2 Just Breathe: Everything Is Perfect Right Now	11
Lesson #3 Build Your Parent Confidence: You Are What You Read, Study, Practice	30
Lesson #4 Your Child's Confidence	45
Lesson #5 Advocate for Your Child: You Get One Chance. Show Up	66
Lesson #6 What's in Your Toolbox? Tips, Organization, Resources	93
Lesson #7 Where Do You Get Your Inspiration? Build Yourself Up	113

Conclusion	122
Collective Wisdom, Cooperative Mindset, and Continuous Learning	
References	125
Acknowledgments	129
About the Author	133
Can You Help?	134

Introduction

"Fishing" Lessons for an Ever-Better Tomorrow

Do what you can, with what you have, where you are. — Teddy Roosevelt

"If you give a man a fish, he will eat for a day. If you teach a man to fish, he can eat for a lifetime." And then, he can teach others to do the same. Like the fisherman, through this book, parents, teachers, and caregivers can cast out their nets into a world of child development knowledge, utilize that learning, and pass it on through the way they guide their children. This is my intention for writing this book—to share what I've learned from my education, experiences, teaching, and resources, to help even just one parent, who in turn will help one child at a time. After all, doesn't everyone want solid life skills, confidence, self-sufficiency, and a better life for their children?

According to Dr. Luis Rojas Marcos, psychiatrist, former professor of psychiatry at New York University's School of Medicine, and New York City's Commissioner of Mental Health, over the past 15 years researchers have provided alarming statistics on the acute and constant increase in childhood mental illness that is now reaching epidemic proportions. For example, one in five children suffer from mental health problems; attention deficit hyperactivity disorder (ADHD) has increased by 43 percent; and teenage depression saw an increase of 37 percent. Combine these statistics with the effects of pandemic schooling and parenting, as well as the negative mental, social, and psychological effects of worldwide mandates related to the pandemic, and the prospective trajectory of mental health problems in the future of children and families appears bleak indeed.

Yet, all is not lost. There is always hope. As a parent, caregiver, or teacher, never ever allow anyone to convince you that your child's growth and development are inevitably negative. This book is a vehicle for hope and a resource for helping you steer your child's future away from negativity and towards positivity.

Victor Frankl, Holocaust survivor, neurologist, psychiatrist, philosopher, and author, explained that everything can be taken from a person except the one last possible control that every human possesses: a person's own thinking, beliefs, or mindset. In Germany's concentration camps of World War II, Victor Frankl, along with millions of others, was stripped of every human dignity and suffered horrific inequities. As a psychologist before and during his imprisonment, he studied, practiced, and taught those around him that although Hitler's fascist reign could take all their physical belongings and cause great suffering to them who were imprisoned in the camps, there was one right the fascists could not take from them without their own permission: the ability to choose their spirit, their mindset, and their outlook on life, as those decisions are always in a person's own control.

My goal and purpose for writing this book is to provide tools so that you can build solid foundations for life in children. The tools I provide equip you to guide children to be caring, truth-seeking, conscientious individuals who have the "I-can-do-anything-I-put-my-mind-to" attitude, confidence, and work ethic. For parents, teachers, and caregivers, life illustrates that it is never too soon or too late to gather the tools needed to start or to continue building up children.

Families cannot assume others outside of the home will lay these foundations in children. Schools, daycare, outside caregivers, etc., help support and add structure, but our children are our responsibility first. If we share and model for children the best of what we have learned, we can help kids make educated decisions throughout life. Empowering new, as well as seasoned, parents, caregivers, and educators to be present and accountable for their childrearing, their child's education, and their child's early interactions outside of school and the home provides the framework for a well-built foundation in children.

Who Is This Book For?

For parents and early childhood educators, raising children can be challenging. New parents want to do everything correctly. No matter a parent or caregiver's age, race, gender, educational background, socioeconomic status, or family history, everyone wants what is best for their children. Human nature provides us this innate desire to love and care for one another, and to value each other. The great big world outside may be a chaotic place, but humanity still maintains the shared inborn psychological attributes of humankind. Nurturing the nature within the immediate cosmos of your own family, one child and one family at a time, across hundreds, thousands, millions, and billions of families, will endow children with the necessary skills as they grow up, thus commissioning them to go out into the world and make it a better place for all.

This book was written to empower the parents and caregivers of young children—young parents, old parents, new first-time parents, and seasoned parents with one or many children, busy parents, and not-so-busy-parents—as well as early childhood professionals and educators.

In addition, this book also was written for the parent who, as a child, did not have a positive school experience and perhaps does not feel comfortable today in a school setting as an adult. For caregivers or parents who did not have supportive parents, or who lived in a family that was uneducated in positive parenting, this book should enlighten you if you so choose. Perhaps you have "imposter syndrome" with regard to parenting, you know, the:

"Who-am-I-to-know-anything-about-parenting-or-sending-my-child-to-school?" complex.

This book is for you!

If you are a parent, caregiver, or educator who wants to learn and grow to become a better parent or teacher, expanding your capacities and capabilities in your own personal parent/teacher world, then this book is for you.

Let's keep in mind: thoughts precede beliefs. You can do anything and learn anything that you put your mind to, focus on, and embrace.

The Book Setup: Lessons and Tools

For your convenience, I have arranged this book into seven easy-to-read lessons that you can read in or out of order, depending on your time availability and the topics that interest you. Feel free to jump ahead and use the information in the order that best suits your parenting, teaching, or caregiving goals. The material will remind you and support you in easy, sound parenting and caregiving guidelines that make sense. After all, sometimes we forget.

Here's a preview of the seven lessons:

- *Lesson #1: Be Present* reminds us that time is fleeting. It provides five simple rules to follow daily for better parent-child relationships and development.

- *Lesson #2: Just Breathe: Everything Is Perfect Right Now* discusses the importance of carefully navigating difficult situations and how to enact positive discipline.

- *Lesson #3: Build Your Parent Confidence: You Are What You Read, Study, Practice* focuses on supporting you, the caregiver, reminding you that you are enough, that observation is a helpful parenting tool, and that being proactive can further build your confidence and skills.

- *Lesson #4: Your Child's Confidence* covers learned behaviors, bullying, and how manners build confidence in children, as well as "building up" all children.

- *Lesson #5: Advocate for Your Child* offers suggestions for

xiii

choosing the right school for your child, as well as covering the topics of nutrition, sleep, babysitters, nannies and daycare, and child safety.

- *Lesson #6: What's in Your Toolbox?* offers extra resources for organizing, routines, and family traditions.

- *Lesson #7: Where Do You Get Your Inspiration? Building Yourself Up to Build Your Child Up* reminds us that in order to build our children up, we must make time for ourselves and offers suggestions.

My Background

My qualifications and inspiration for writing this book derive from my time studying early childhood development, my career teaching preschool, kindergarten, and first grade, and my own parenting experiences. During my teaching career, I worked with hundreds of children and their families, each one of them unique and exquisite.

In the rest of this section on my background, I will share special milestones on my journey towards embracing and advocating children and leadership in the area of early childhood development, starting with the one that first opened the door for me—or rather, that I discovered upon opening a door.

I was living in Chicago and working in public relations. One morning, as I was headed out the door of my brownstone apartment building, I had a life-changing experience. When I opened the front door, there was a smelly pile of grungy clothes lying on the vestibule floor, blocking my ability to exit. Startled, I quickly realized that the clothes pile actually was a body, and one that did not move even with the opening of the loud and heavy old door. I immediately thought, "Dead person." Naturally, I freaked out, shut the loud, creaking door, and quickly locked the heavy deadbolt. Still, there was no movement.

After the police showed up, I could hear the thankfully alive homeless man saying, "You can't do that, I paid for that," as the officers poured out the mouthwash that the gentleman had used to intoxicate himself. I still can hear those words today. The poor fellow looked as if he was 80 years old. Sadly, I learned that he was just 22.

The entire incident stuck with me. I just kept thinking, "How could a young man of 22 end up in this terrible situation at such a young age? Who are his parents, his siblings, his friends? Where are they today? And more importantly, how did this young adult end up homeless, dirty, and drunk on my doorstep? What direction and support systems were lacking in this former child's life?"

Shortly after the disturbing event, I decided to do something more rewarding with my career in hopes that maybe I could help prevent one child from ending up in this same young homeless man's situation. I had already earned my BA in communications and public address, so back to school I went for a Master of Arts in Early Childhood Education. The early childhood program I pursued focused on childhood development from birth through third grade.

In addition to every academic and child development learning course in the program, I learned the most important concept from a professor who also worked in the Robert Taylor Homes Chicago Projects low-income housing. The teacher always reminded us that everyone loves their children, explaining, "Always remember the single mom or drug addict or the poor family may look like they don't care, but they truly do love their children. Many of those humans just didn't have a good example growing up." She went on to explain, "Never judge a book by its cover. Everyone has baggage. Always remember and consider the love and the possible baggage with every child and family you serve."

While working on my master's degree, I taught at a wonderful private preschool located just east of the L tracks and the Cabrini Green Chicago Projects, a low-income housing complex. Teaching young three-year-olds was a blessing in many ways. I loved the wonder and joy the toddlers exhibited. Young children maintain the gifts of observation, innocence, and delight. Youth notice the world differently than adults.

One of my students, Abby, was standing in front of a large glass window, looking out from within our classroom and staring off into the car-filled parking lot when she said, "Look at all of those beautiful mufflers." Then we both laughed. How does a three-year-old child notice mufflers on over one hundred cars, in a parking lot, in front of the L tracks with Cabrini Green Projects in the background? And what makes them "beautiful" to a three-year-old?

When I shared the story with her parents, they informed me that the family owned a car repair shop, so the comment made sense, but still the concept that she noticed and commented on the mufflers instead of something else was intriguing.

Another toddler named Michael walked outside to play and commented, "Boy, Miss Margaret, the sky is so blue today." Isn't it beautiful and joyful that children notice their surroundings and fine details, such as mufflers and an azure blue sky, even in the midst of city life?

Teaching preschool while working towards a master's was incredibly rewarding and educational. My non-speaking three-year-old student, Thomas, suffered from developmental dyspraxia but was one of the happiest children in the class. We worked on making sounds and practicing facial exercises provided by his speech pathologist. One day while eating snack, he looked me straight in the eye, proceeded to throw up all over, and slowly forced sound from his tiny lips, speaking his first word, "M-o-o-o-o-o-m."

"Thomas, you said your first word, 'Mom'!" I said with excitement and gratefulness. Despite the fact that he was sick, Thomas, his mother, and I were overjoyed by his speaking. That day, like every other day spent teaching, was extremely rewarding.

Just because teaching is rewarding does not mean the profession is easy. Teachers and parents must keep their communication lines open so that both parties have the best intentions, knowledge, and support of students. I learned the importance of parent-teacher communication when a parent came to speak with me about her son. The mother said, "Please do not tell my son NOT to hit back. We live in a rough area of Chicago, and he must learn to protect himself." I was grateful for her insight and communication. Her family's situation had never even crossed my mind. The mother and I worked together to address the situation in the classroom without lowering the importance of the child's ability to self-defend in his neighborhood. The situation taught me that I can always continue learning more about my students, as well as continue working with parents to accommodate situations that arise.

My time teaching preschool was rewarding in a multitude of ways and laid a foundation for continuing my education and growth as a teacher. The simple joy of every child in my path while teaching preschool was a daily gift for which I am forever grateful.

Once I earned my master's, I was hired to teach first grade in a suburb of Chicago. On the first day of school, I had to physically restrain a six-year-old student while reading the book *Brown Bear, Brown Bear*. The first-grade children were quietly seated on the carpet in front of my reading chair. A six-year-old boy from a seated position on the floor aggressively reached up onto a nearby desk and picked up a freshly sharpened pencil. The boy screamed, "I am going to kill you, I am going to stab each one of you!"

The five- and six-year-old classmates in my care went silent, their eyes widened, and they began looking away from the boy holding the now dagger-like pencil. And like the parting of the Red Sea, the students slowly backed away, leaving only the boy and me alone in the center. There was an eerie silence. Even the little first graders knew in their souls that something was wrong. So, as to never create fear, I spoke calmly to the boy as my heart raced ferociously within my chest. In the back of my mind, I remembered that I had been trained for this type of situation in my early childhood program. Thus, I employed the second most useful concept I learned from that amazing master's professor mentioned earlier. To protect students from an aggressive child, we were taught to safely restrain a child who is posing a serious danger and potential risk to himself and those around him. In doing so, I softly spoke to the enraged child, "You are safe. No one will hurt you, and you will hurt no one."

Keeping this long, sad story short, unfortunately, the child had to be removed permanently from the first grade class for safety reasons. The school learned that he had come from an abusive home life, had threatened several babysitters with knives and scissors, and lived with siblings who exhibited similar behaviors. All the walls in his home had holes that had been bashed in by force. The heartbreaking tale of this child and others like him is a reminder that we do not know everyone's family situation or the life a child lives outside of the classroom. Be kind, be helpful, and be supportive to all children and families.

After a year of teaching first grade, a kindergarten teaching position became available in the same school. My mother had been a kindergarten teacher, and that was the grade I had always wanted to teach, so I graciously accepted the position with enthusiasm. One of the best teaching techniques I learned at the wonderful school in which I worked was the kindergarten conference. Every year in the fall on the day before school started, the kindergarten teachers held kindergarten conferences. The activity was a phenomenal way to start the kindergarten school year. Parents signed up ahead of time to attend their very own 30-minute conference with the teacher. A parent could choose to bring their incoming kindergartener to the meeting, or if the caregiver felt it was important to discuss the child without the student in the room, that parent could choose not to bring their child. More often than not, the child attended the conference with their parents.

The individual conference visit, held during a quiet, non-school day, helped the young children transition into regular school. As teachers, we felt strongly that the child having the opportunity to ease into the school year, during a pre-visit to the school and classroom (accompanied by their parent or caregiver) best supported each child's comfort zone; the interaction helped reduce the anxiety students often experienced on the actual first day of kindergarten. The visit allowed the child to familiarize themselves with the classroom, play, ask questions, etc.

While the child explored and played, we, teachers and caregivers, discussed the child's background and completed a questionnaire together. Some questions on the list included: *Do you have any concerns that your child is not ready for kindergarten, and if so, what are they? What does your child enjoy doing at home? Does your child have siblings? Will your child take the bus, or will you or a caregiver pick up your child at school? Who is authorized to pick up your child at school? How do you handle discipline in your family? What is the best way to contact parents/caregivers?*

The pre-kindergarten conference was a wonderful way to open the lines of communication between the teacher and the parents, as well as provide a comfortable introduction to kindergarten for the child. I cannot stress enough how beneficial this strategy was for the parents and the teachers, thus making the first day of kindergarten a much more positive experience for everyone. If you are a teacher, offer a pre-kindergarten conference to your students each year; the extra time put into hosting a pre-kindergarten conference will truly benefit your students, your classroom, and the parents you serve.

People who know me and with whom I have taught and worked recognize that I have a soft spot for all children, but especially the troublemakers, the non-parented kids, the children with loving parents who perhaps grew up without positive parenting, and the children whose parents are new to parenting and still learning. Sometimes during growth and development, the wonder in small children can get lost if it is not nurtured and celebrated. All children, no matter their background, home life or parents, deserve to be nurtured, celebrated, educated, guided, and loved.

My husband and I raised daughters. During preschool, we moved so that our children could attend a better child-centered elementary school district that provided half-day kindergarten. One of our daughters was bullied, and as a result, we changed schools again and moved homes for the betterment of our children. Moving and leaving a wonderful neighborhood and old friends full of hardworking families, stay-at-home dads with working moms, and traditional and non-traditional families was very difficult. In the old neighborhood, kids played outside, not on computers or before TVs. Summer, fall, winter, and spring children and families spent most of their time outdoors, exploring, learning, enjoying, and growing. Changing schools and neighborhoods was not easy; however, because moving was in the best interest of our children, we were willing to move. We made those tough decisions as a family. The moves paid off and our children's experiences, both academically and socially, were positive and perfect for our family. While growing up, our children attended public and private preschools, grade schools, high schools, colleges, and universities.

I invite you to consider what I have learned through my experiences as a teacher and parent. I do not claim to be an expert. Every day, every experience, and every moment provide opportunities for each of us to learn more. I continue to build my knowledge through a variety of experiences such as teaching in various capacities, as well as taking in information from multi-media sources, books, articles, documentaries, podcasts, etc.

My hope is that all children grow into responsible, kind, and self-sufficient adults. If one tiny anecdote, story, suggestion, or resource from this book helps you become a better parent, teacher, or caregiver, so you, in turn, can better guide your child to grow into a confident, conscientious human being, then this book will have served the purpose for which it was written.

Lesson #1

Be Present: You Never Get This Time Back

I've learned that people will forget what you said, people will forget what you did, but people will never forget how you made them feel. — Maya Angelou

First and foremost, parents need to "be present" for their children. Science tells us that subconsciously, all humans desire support in the form of time spent with loved ones, attention, and acceptance. Children are no exception. Developmentally, children inherently require proof, through caregiver actions, that the adult is in control of all situations involving the child and that the adult loves them and will always be available and supportive of them.

Positive parental time spent with children from an early age on helps establish in children a solid foundation and concept of self, as well as builds self-confidence. Building a positive sense of self in a child—meaning they feel fully supported, loved, and capable—is a foundation that will support them for a lifetime. When children feel completely supported through "present" parenting, self-confidence is fostered, which helps build the beginnings of a child's character and sense of self. How do children subconsciously know and learn these supported feelings? Through their parents'/caregivers' actions. Simply explained, when you are with your children, really be there for them, both physically and mentally. Be present. Stay engaged and focused and make a point to enjoy the big and the little moments together.

Everyone says, "Oh, time goes so quickly, and children grow up way too fast." Unfortunately, this realization usually does not occur to parents until their children are all grown up rather than when the children are younger. This progression is understandable. When parents or caregivers are in the exhausting, yet wonderful, baby and toddler stage, often they are tired and cannot see light at the end of the tunnel. Thus, the thought of kids growing up quickly never enters the mind. Even still, when you find yourself wanting to disengage and do the easy thing, instead of doing the right thing, try to remember to tell yourself, "I will never get this time back with my children, so I am going to enjoy this special moment and be grateful." Be present and connect emotionally when your children are talking and when you are spending time together. Smile, kiss, play, read, dance, jump, and play some more! You never, ever get this "together time" back. Carpe diem! Seize the day.

In the rest of this chapter, you'll find simple tools that provide more options for ensuring that you and other adult caregivers are present for your children and that this sacred attention that you give, and your children receive, is enjoyed daily. Among the topics you will find are a weekly family meeting, rules around devices and screen time, family dinners, and more.

Scheduled Family Time

How do you picture your family as it evolves over time? Will your family be close-knit, conducting activities together as your children grow up? When your small children are teens and young adults, will they then make space in their schedules to spend time with your family? If you want your family to value and learn that family time, the time when the entire family is together and present, is important, then you must schedule, practice, and model this concept from your family's very beginning. Children learn through experience and observations. Prioritize family time and teach children through experiences that they are an important part of the whole family and that family comes first. Maintaining and supporting "hallowed" family time is equally important to child development as the practice teaches little children the simple value of siblings and parents, which helps foster the idea that we must make time for others, in addition to ourselves. It has been said that "a family that plays togethers, stays together."

To help your family make the most of their time together, discuss the importance of family time with your loved ones or fellow caregivers. Together, create a plan that works best for your own specific family and each person's activities and timetables. Look at your schedules, review your calendars and your day. Then, on a weekly basis, host a family meeting where you, the children, and the other adult(s) meet to set and share schedules, in order to determine when everyone can be together for family time. What works for you, your spouse, or fellow guardians? What activities do the children have this week?

Scheduling family time on the calendar highlights the importance of family togetherness and allows families to say, "no" to less important activities or to schedule them at a different time. Programming family time on the calendar also helps families determine what activities are most important and valuable to their own inner circle.

In addition to creating a schedule, the weekly family meeting is beneficial for celebrating weekly successes and accomplishments, discussing family issues and solutions, meal planning requests, gratefulness rituals, general reminders, game nights, or family activity night—whatever topics your family believes should be addressed and conducted during that time. More about family meeting activities later in this lesson.

Device Rules

Real, direct human interaction seems to have lost its importance in our tech-savvy world. It is important to note here that all caregivers should be aware of the many negative effects that technical device usage—devices such as computers, phones, tablets—and their glowing screens have on children. In *Glow Kids: How Screen Addiction is Hijacking Our Kids—and How to Break the Trance*, author Nicholas Kardaras provides findings from research that studied the imaging of children's brains when the children were watching glowing screens. All screens, especially when excessively used, produce dopamine-activating factors that can neurologically damage a young person's developing brain in the same way as a cocaine addiction. For example, when a cell phone pings, dopamine hits the brain, as a result of the screen's glow. When measurements are taken in the brain, the areas of the cranium light up in a way that is very similar to the effect of cocaine on the brain. The continuous dopamine hits go on to condition that person or child's brain to become addicted. The finding: children can become addicted to the screen. Addictive behaviors in young children may, later in life, further develop to include addictions to food, drugs, alcohol, risky behaviors, etc.

Unfortunately, society is very slow to acknowledge the harmful effects of screen time. I highly recommend that you do your own research and decide how much time you will allow your child to play on a computer, tablet, or phone. To inform yourself on how seriously damaging screen time is for your children, I suggest that you read *Dopamine Nation* by Anna Lembke or watch the 2020 docudrama entitled *The Social Dilemma*. Be advised that the statistics and material are alarming; however, the valuable information can act as a resource for you as a parent.

When the situation arises, choose active play or non-tech activities rather than using technology to babysit your children even though screen time will seem the easier option. Think about the effects that the screen time will have on your child's brain. Ask yourself whether playing with toys or playing on a screened device is more beneficial to your child's health and human development.

It's critical you remember that your children learn how to behave from watching you. Therefore, it is not only about creating device rules for your children, but also for yourself when you are with them. When you are with your children, focus on your child. Be present to them. Enjoy the gift of time together. Model attentive behavior. Be positive, and set a good example through your own intentional behavior. Do not set a negative example for your children by living life as a digitally distracted parent. Focus on your children during family time, dinner, or anytime you are together. Later, when they are old enough to use a device of their own, they will have already experienced your good example, and it will be easier for them to give you the same presence, attention, and respect. In this way, you are fostering a real relationship with your child starting at an early age, and at the same time, keeping both your brains healthier as well.

I recommend that you decide as a family to create a family pact: no cell phones, computers, tablets, or televisions in use during dinner or while the caregivers are with the children. The no-cell-phone-computer-and-tablet rule also should apply to the time you spend with your spouse, other family members, or anyone else. Think about it—when was the rule implemented entitling the phone, computer, or television to be more important than the people with whom you spend the most time?

Daily Connection and Play Time: Free and Guided

To help connect with your children, you do not have to take them on fancy vacations or field trips, sign them up for the latest classes, or buy them the newest toys. Instead, pay attention to what they enjoy doing, and do those activities with them. Take the time. Seize the moment together. If they enjoy reading, read with them. If coloring or crafting is their love, get messy and create or draw with them. Play outside, run, jump, pretend; whatever your child wants to play, play that with them!

Lead by example. If they are playing with cars, ask them, "What are you doing?" When they answer, say to them, "Tell me more about that" or "Tell me about your cars." Be grateful that you can take the time to learn about your child's interests. Remember, time is fleeting.

Setting aside just 20 to 30 minutes each day strictly for parent-child connecting can be very rewarding for both you and your child. If necessary, schedule this time on your daily calendar. The time spent together is an opportunity for you as a parent, teacher, or caregiver to observe the child's play behaviors, verbal skills, eye contact, and general age-appropriate developmental and socialization skills. The exercise may feel like an interruption or a slowdown of your day, but the time spent being present and mindful, as well as observing your child's behaviors, can be helpful if you have child development concerns.

In addition, spending concentrated play time with your children simply provides a positive connection and family bond with your child. Focusing your time engaging and playing with your child is not only rewarding but informative should you or teachers have concerns about age-appropriate behaviors and milestones. Meaningful play with your children also helps when you feel disconnected from your own child or those youth in your care. Play may feel awkward because you are an adult; however, play is an integral part in every child's development.

As stated in the Association for Psychological Science's article, "Guided Play Principles and Practices": "Decades of research have shown that free play is necessary for [children's] healthy development and can boost certain skills in early childhood." Free play is exactly what it sounds like: a child playing freely, playing however and whatever they choose.

While daily connection with your children through play is important, do not feel responsible for always keeping your children occupied and entertained. Instead, provide opportunities for boredom and self-direction as that is when creativity comes alive. Whether conducted within your home or outside, together, or alone, play helps build a child's brain development through exploration, imagination, discovery, and interaction with others. Playing constructs in children the foundation for turn-taking, problem solving, human growth, communication, and self-confidence.

Guided play, often found in early childhood education practices, combines the best elements of free play and direct instruction when an educational end goal is desired. Families also can use guided play for homeschooling, as well as teaching specific concepts. All play, whether free or guided, together or alone, helps develop social, emotional, mental, and physical qualities in children.

Family Dinner

Schedules vary from family to family and child to child. All families are busy. Be sure to make time for dinner together as a family at least one night a week, and ideally, if possible, every evening. Get back to the basics. Remember, no TV or cell phones. Discuss the current day's activities or plans for the weekend. Talk about what you are grateful for from that day.

The practice of discussing at the dinner table is helpful for children learning to speak, learning to make eye contact, and learning the vocal turn-taking concept of questioning and answering. Children learn to take turns during dinner table discussions. Believe it or not, these situations are where your child begins building the foundations for speaking in class, taking turns when speaking, answering questions, and eventually public speaking. All that and it starts at the dinner table. Who knew?

Every parent, caregiver, and teacher desires polite children who grow up into polite adults. The simple turn-taking and speaking exercise that happens through discussion around the family dinner table is great for children, as well as a wonderful reminder for adults. If you need help in this area or just want to introduce a new learning concept, there are fun, non-tech dinner games and age-appropriate conversation starter cards available at bookstores and online. Perhaps, you can think back to your childhood for verbal turn-taking games to share with your family.

Promises and Follow-Through

Families and parents are busy. You work, you cook, you clean, you cut the grass and do laundry, you carpool—yada, yada, yada. Everyone is busy. Make time for your children! Be present! Every day is a gift—the good, the bad, and the ugly. Plan ahead and schedule time on your calendar, write out family activities, and stick to your calendar commitments. All these actions help you to be more present with your children and family. With that said, it is equally important to be accountable for the commitments you make to your children. Being present means that you follow through with what you tell your children you will do with them. Do not tell your children that you will do something for which you have no time or that you know you cannot participate in and accomplish. This broken promise and lack-of-follow-through behavior teaches children that it is okay to say one thing but do another.

Non-dependable parent, teacher, and caregiver behavior is not okay. Repetitive let-down situations such as these set children up for failure for their entire lives. Children learn through experience. If a child is regularly being let down by a parent who promises one thing, but does not follow through, or always provides something other than what was originally promised, the child learns that their parent/caregiver is not dependable. Even worse, the child learns to repeat the non-dependable behavior because they never learn how to be accountable. The vicious cycle sets a child up for not following through with friends, school, homework, group projects etc.

When adults are accountable and follow through with promises and schedules, children learn accountability and trust. If you tell your child you will play with them after work, plan play time into your schedule.

Utilize your calendar. If you find it helpful, set a timer, and explain to your child that you can play for a certain amount of time. After that time, then you must work for a certain amount of time. Explaining to young children that the time you will be working is only temporary and that your work has an end time helps children understand that the delay in play is not forever. A digital and/or traditional clock photo-printed or drawn on a piece of paper identifying when you will be done, and can play again, acts as an easy and simple prop. Give the clock image to your child and explain that when the clock looks the same as your picture, that is when you will be ready to play and spend time with them. The time clock activity allows the child to have concrete evidence of when you will be available, as well as acting as the beginning teachings of the concept of time.

Later in life, when you look back at your many years as a parent, teacher, or caregiver, and you think about how you raised your children, will you be able to say with true conviction that you were genuinely present for those individuals in your care? Did you schedule family time and follow through with the commitments you made to your family and children? Did you make time to have dinner as a family? Did you help your children foster good behavior through your own positive behaviors? No one wants to reflect on their own lives and their years of child-rearing with regret. There is no time like the present to "be present" for your children and genuinely invest your time in their futures. Because this is real life we are talking about, there will be challenges and discontent at times when the family is together, and that brings us to the topic of the next chapter, which is all about handling those challenges when they arise.

Lesson #2

Just Breathe: Everything Is Perfect Right Now

You can't go back and change the beginning, but you can start where you are and change the ending. — C.S. Lewis

Now that you have decided to "be present," as given in the first lesson, what will you do when "life happens" or poor behaviors get in the way? Just breathe. Why do that? Because everything is perfect, just the way it is.

Reality is happening right now, whether you like it or not. Reality is now, not the past, not the future, but rather—right now. Your life, everyone's life, is perfect at this very moment. In your mind, your situation may not feel ideal at this moment, but you are positioned where you are supposed to be—right where you are—in your current state of affairs. We humans are part of a cosmos that is much grander than we know. For some reason, wherever we find ourselves, we are supposed to be right where we are, right now.

Certain choices and behaviors may or may not have affected how you arrived at your current position. Regardless of how you got where you are now or whether the situation is positive, negative, or somewhere in between, you are where you are presently, so breathe deeply and embrace life. Just breathe.

Consider that you and your child and your spouse or anyone with you at this exact moment have been put into one another's lives, and life is perfect. In your frustration, you may not think that life is perfect. Stop, breathe, and practice this skill: when situations are challenging, look at the other person or child, take a deep breath, and think to yourself, "I am supposed to grow from this irritating event [or this poor behavior]." Employ this method to remove the emotion, energy, and/or anger out of the situation. "I am right where I am supposed to be right now. My child is right where they are supposed to be right now. These events are happening because they are happening. Good or bad, the obstacles I am [or we are] facing are the current reality. How do the issues help me [or my child] grow and learn? Even with these issues, how can I show up with grace?"

All caregivers must be good examples for the children under their wings. After all, children learn how to manage themselves when facing challenges based on how they see their caregivers manage themselves in similar situations. When you make mistakes and your behavior is not perfect, utilize grace to let go of the attempted power grab, and say to your child [or spouse or whoever is involved], "I am sorry that I lost my temper" or "This is a difficult time, but we will get through it. We will be stronger in the long run for having gone through this difficult situation."

In the rest of this chapter, we explore more ways that you can better handle difficult situations that will arise. We further discuss how you can guide your children to make positive behavior choices and how greatly your own behavior choices act as the template for your children's behaviors. From effectively teaching your children good etiquette, to best handling chores and children's understanding of money, to "catching them doing something good" to reinforce positive behaviors—this chapter equips you to accept the present moment as perfect, even when it is messy, to make the most of the present moment, and to just breathe while you are guiding your child, and yourself, to make better and more positive behavior choices.

Handling Difficult Situations and Discipline—It's A Must

Life is as it is right now. Sometimes life will feel easy and run smoothly, and other times there will be bumps in the road. We are given one life. There will be challenges, especially when it comes to parenting. As a parent, you have many options on how to handle difficult situations and correct poor behavior with your children. Do your research on different discipline methods. In Angela Duckworth's book *Grit—The Power of Passion and Perseverance*, the author discusses grit plus wise parenting versus not-so-wise parenting. Duckworth states:

> Over the past 40 years, study after carefully designed study has found that the children of psychologically wise parents fare better than children raised in any other kind of household. In one of Larry's studies, for example, about ten thousand American teenagers completed questionnaires about their parents' behavior. Regardless of gender, ethnicity, social class, or parents' marital status, teens with warm, respectful, and demanding parents

earned higher grades in school, were more self-reliant, suffered from less anxiety and depression, and were less likely to engage in delinquent behavior.

Duckworth defines the virtue of "wise psychological parenting" as parents who are both warm and demanding, have high standards, and provide total support. The authoritarian parenting method exhibits high standards and demands, but provides low to little warmth. On the other hand, permissive parents have high warmth, but low standards. Sadly, neglectful parents have neither. What parenting method will you choose to employ: wise, authoritarian, permissive, or neglectful?

Recently at the hair salon, I listened to a lovely lady speaking with her banker about whose name was on the bank account. When she hung up the phone, the woman proceeded to tell her own heart-breaking story. She had been divorced for about three years. Her sons were seven, 14, and 16 years old, and the children lived part-time in separate households in the same town. Half the week they spent with the mother while the second half played out with the other parent. The woman was distraught and said her boys were terribly disrespectful to her, and they often spoke unkindly to her. Her sad story sounded like a bad movie.

The lady's parents had sold their own home in Canada, in an effort to obtain the financial means to buy their daughter's home. The grandparents' purchase of the daughter's home allowed their grandsons and their mother to remain in the family home in which the boys had grown up. There was one hitch—the grandparents would be living with this mother and her three sons. This distressing story gets worse. Not only were the children disrespectful to the mother, but also to the grandparents. Worst of all, the 14-year-old boy was stealing money from his mother's wallet on the days that she received her work pay. The mother did not realize that the boy was stealing until some time had passed and she noticed that she was low on cash. Sadly, the boy was not stealing the money for himself, rather he was raiding substantial amounts of cash and giving it to his father, the ex-husband, who had been asking his son to take these dishonest actions.

My first thought was, "Oh, what a sad situation. What is this father teaching his young teenage son? Dishonesty, stealing, disrespect? What terrible feelings does the boy have when he pilfers from his mother's purse because his father has asked him to steal? How will this dishonest behavior and the boy's own guilt affect him as he grows into adulthood?" And the list goes on.

Stressed out, the mother was in the salon for a quick wash and style, and was in a hurry, as her other son, the 16-year-old, had forgotten his lunch and snack that day. Apparently, this mistake happened regularly, and the mom was often interrupted with the same request, even during her workday. Did you notice I wrote that the boy was 16?

Before I delve into accountability and point out that a well-functioning 16-year-old boy should be able to remember his lunch and snack, and the fact that he is definitely way too old to have his mom bring his forgotten lunch repeatedly, let us think about how a family gets to this crazed state in the first place. This "forgot-my-snack-and-lunch" behavior is not a problem if it happens every once in a while. However, if this is a recurring event, a family needs to take appropriate action to help their child learn how to manage remembering their lunch/snack (or any other age-appropriate responsibility). What if there was no one to bring food to school? Would the teen go hungry? Maybe. Might the boy decide to pack a lunch the next day? Perhaps. Could this event be used as a learning tool? Absolutely.

Every parent can sympathize with this "forgot-my-lunch" ordeal. In this situation, the mother has underlying guilt stemming from the divorce. She wants her children to be happy and fed, and she wants them to like her. The mom, like everyone else, is human. Innately, parents desire happiness, ease, goodness, etc., for their children ... always. These are wonderful traits that humans possess. The problem in this situation arises from feelings of guilt. The mother thinks she is doing what is best for her 16-year-old son by bringing his lunch. She wants him to be happy and to show him she loves him, and the action makes the mother feel good about making her son happy. And that is a normal way of thinking. However, as parents, sometimes it is important to step out of your own state of affairs and say to yourself in a situation like this, "Is what I am doing [in this case, repeatedly bringing my 16-year-old son his lunch] helping my child become a competent, self-sufficient young adult? Or is my behavior holding back their learning to be independent?"

Something to think about—how will this young man remember to bring lunch to work or college when he is older? This little bit of tough love is hard as a parent, but you must think of it as helping raise your child to be better able to take care of themselves.

So, what is the purpose of this teenager's story, and why are you reading it in an early childhood parenting book? All too often you hear stories like this, and you think this awful incident would never occur in your family. Positive, wise parenting and discipline should start when your children are toddlers. Waiting to teach and expect good behavior until your children are adolescents will be more stressful for both the child and the parent.

I included this story to remind parents and caregivers that it is your job to set up your children for success, not failure, from the very beginning. You are the parent. You must handle discipline and difficult situations when children are young. Choose grit, passion, and perseverance when guiding your children and utilize wise-parenting strategies that are demanding, yet provide warmth, establish high standards, but are totally supportive of your children. And, don't forget to breathe. Remember, everything is perfect, you are constantly learning, and you are doing your best!

Empower your children to take care of themselves from the very beginning. Be logical and age-appropriate in what you teach your children and in the good behaviors and responsibilities you expect from them as they grow. Exemplifying and illustrating honesty and character through your own behavior, as well as making "the right choice over the easy choice" are life lessons every caregiver should pass on to their offspring. Nothing is more important in life than helping children become better versions of themselves.

When adults work to become better versions of themselves day in and day out, they can build the same rewarding habits in their own children. Teach kids skills and behaviors that will help them "control the controllables" as they grow up. Think about appropriate redirection of poor behaviors, life-skills teachings, and age-appropriate discipline as helping kids grow to be independent, self-sufficient, caring adolescents, teens, and young adults. Choose wise parenting over authoritarian, permissive, and neglectful parenting. And just ask yourself, heaven forbid, if something ever happened to you or your spouse, what basic skills would help your child help themselves, "control the controllables," or simply ease their survival? Surely, these simple, yet important life skills are what you want your children to learn: self-discipline, self-care, appropriate social skills, interactive problem-solving tactics, personal hygiene, healthy eating, organizational skills, a good work ethic, kindness, honesty, and doing the right thing, not the easy thing.

The great Lou Holtz in his book, *Winning Every Day*, said, "Discipline is not something you do to yourself; it is something you do for yourself. Without self-discipline, we can't make appropriate choices." He continues, "A disciplinarian is someone who requires that people understand the consequences of their decisions." Teach your children, starting at an early age, right from wrong, explaining the consequences that will result from making poor choices. Discipline is different from punishment in that discipline informs the child of the consequences of poor behavior. "Offenders choose punishment by their actions," Holtz states. Distilling discipline within ourselves and teaching our children discipline holds all involved parties accountable for their actions and behaviors. Teaching and expecting accountability in your children will help build their character, empowering them to become accountable adolescents, teens, and adults.

Fostering Positive Behavior

Spending time with your children and fostering positive behaviors and kindness starting at an early age has life-enhancing effects. Actively teach your children how to recognize and handle their own frustrations and anger. Actively demonstrate and practice social skills and self-regulation skills, including how to greet others, how to take turns, how to share without being left without anything, how to say please and thank you, how to recognize mistakes, and how to say, "sorry" when necessary. Actively teach children the ever-important life skill of patience, the ability to wait. Aim to foster their aptitude for delayed gratification.

Emotionally available parents set clear boundaries for good behavior and expected responsibilities. There are a million books, websites, articles, videos, and podcasts floating around on simple ways to acknowledge and foster good behavior in children. The early childhood education and parenting sections online and in bookstores have a wealth of ideas. Here is just one example: on a weekly basis, take one photo of your child doing something you love seeing them do or exhibiting a positive behavior. Print the photo, and on the back of the paper, write a positive comment for the child. This activity is easy considering the plethora of smartphones on the market today.

If you cannot take pictures, no problem; take the technology out of the equation, and go back to the basics. Perhaps you can simply write a positive acknowledgement note, e.g., "Alexandra, I loved watching you help your brother put his toys away."

Each Sunday at dinner or during your family meeting, read the note or notes to the children, and put the positive note, with or without the photo, into a notebook for the child to keep and look at often.

The purpose of this is to get kids thinking about doing good, helping others, and valuing positive actions. When children watch their parents do something good, they learn to model that positive behavior. (Equally important is the fact that the same outcome is true when children observe negative behaviors from their caregivers, i.e., it encourages them to model the same negative behaviors.)

When parents notice and commend children while "catching them doing something good" (later in this chapter we discuss this more), the children then begin to notice the behavior in others. Ideally, the concept helps reinforce good behavior. Please note, this practice does not support complimenting every single behavior. Some behaviors are expected. Do not turn this activity into a disingenuous experience. Parents can go overboard with the concept. Instead, be logical and authentic in your positive reinforcement when "catching them doing something good."

Another example to help promote positive behavior would be to ask each child what they are grateful for during dinner each night. The list could be recorded through voice recordings or written down and stored in a "gratefulness jar" that you all decorate. On weekends, the whole family can look back at the week's gratefulness jar or book, or listen to the voice recordings.

Being grateful for simple things can have a calming effect on everyone involved. What are you grateful for today? Was it the sparkling white snow, the crisp wintry air, or the blue sky? Maybe you are grateful for simply having dinner together. What good deed were you caught doing this week? The question-and-answer options are endless.

Mold this activity to best fit your individual family. The collection of book pages or voice recordings serves as a keepsake for parents but also a reminder of the simplicity of a child's thoughts and the importance of time spent together as a family. When your children are grown and out of the house, you will treasure these recordings and special "out-of-the-mouths-of-babes" utterances from your children. Teaching children to be thankful, grateful, and kind at an early age—and really any age—can help build a child's concept of self, self-esteem, and self-worth.

No "If-Then" Reward Systems

Daily actions such as brushing your teeth, washing your hands, and bathing are necessary skills for life. These sorts of womb-to-tomb routines are integral for health and longevity in all humans. Young children need direction and assistance in these areas so that they learn to take good, proper care of themselves as they age. Life skill topics are off the table when it comes to rewards, allowance, etc. Do not give rewards for expected self-hygiene, such as brushing teeth. If you think about it, that concept is truly silly. What is logical about rewarding anyone for taking care of themselves or preventing their teeth from decaying and falling out through the use of toothpaste and a toothbrush?

Remember, think logically about these situations and take the emotion out. Every human needs to learn personal hygiene, and this learning starts when people are toddlers. There should be no bargaining when it comes to self-care. Do not say to your toddler, "If you brush your teeth, then you get to play." Remember, no "if-then" discipline. Learn to rephrase and redirect the behavior by saying, "When [after, as soon as, etc.] you brush your teeth, we will read a story [watch a program]." This rephrasing takes practice, yet it is far more effective since linguistically the restructured speech informs the child that they will be brushing their teeth and puts the emphasis on a fun activity following the child's completion of the task.

Be conscious of how and what you are asking or telling your children. Make it a game in your head and say to yourself, "I will try to say x-y-z, the next time that I am trying to redirect my child's behavior to the action [or positive behavior] I want them to exhibit." Taking care of their bodies should be expected, not rewarded. Learning the self-care concept is simple for children if parents teach them how and why and make the process enjoyable and expected.

Food Rewards = Negative Consequences

Withholding food or rewarding certain behaviors with food are two discipline strategies that should never be used. Using food in this way may seem harmless at a young age, but when practiced regularly, hard-to-break eating disorders such as anorexia, binging and purging, bulimia, and weight issues may result in your child. Life is difficult enough for children, teens, and adults without life-threatening health matters centered around food. Choose more positive behavior redirection practices mentioned throughout this book instead of food rewards.

Rethinking Allowances

When you were growing up, you may have known some families that gave weekly allowances. Today, that tradition continues in some homes. Take a moment to consider rethinking and changing this "allowance concept"; instead, utilize a "contract concept" for chores.

Back in the day, allowance was essentially money or goods given on a weekly basis similar to a stipend. Unless there were specific tasks to be completed, and a taskmaster like Mom or Dad to keep track of jobs, it may have been easier to just pass a few bucks to the kids each week as an allowance or weekly stipend. Think about the construct. Were kids learning the important concept that work produces rewards? Probably not because allowances lack accountability unless the taskmaster is "on their game" that week.

The real-world American dream was created on the basis that work would be rewarded with payment. The more you worked, the more money you would make, assuming you followed a conscientious budget and savings plan. The great country that you live in continues to allow everyone to follow the principles upon which the United States was founded. Adults go to work, and in response, workers earn a paycheck; you earn a living; you make money. Simply said, working and earning a paycheck allows people to pay for their basic human needs: shelter, food, utilities, transportation, etc. If you want your children to grow up understanding this concept and desiring a better, financially fulfilling, and stable life, rethink the allowance or "weekly stipend," which likely doesn't reinforce the concept.

Empowering children from an early age with the concept that working reaps rewards is a skill that will stay with them throughout life. Simply said in business terms, think "contract of services for payment," instead of weekly stipend or allowance. Determine age-appropriate tasks, write them down, and discuss what compensation you and the child agree upon or work towards (stickers, pennies, activities—whatever you and the client, your child, decide).

Learning about Work

Perhaps Mom works out of the house or Dad works from home. Children learn quickly if you explain in simple terms the definition of work and explain, again in simple terms, your type of work. In addition, explaining why you work can be a good learning experience for children of any age. During pretend play, children often buy food from a grocery store or fill up their play car with gas. To buy the play food or gas for their mini-car, they pay the salesperson.

Play time is a great opportunity to teach lessons about work and earning a living. Now do not overdo the lesson. Remember, this is play time. When children are curious about working and of the appropriate age, they become inquisitive. That time of curiosity is a great opportunity to introduce the work or contract concept, rather than a weekly allowance. Of course, and of equal importance, is that when you say "work," the task must be age-appropriate. Perhaps the dog needs to be brushed regularly, or Mom needs help in the kitchen sorting the silverware out of the dishwasher.

If your child wants to participate in your home's economic structure, then use the opportunity for teaching. You, the parent, and the child decide what job or task you believe is age-appropriate and feasible, according to your child's age and abilities. Depending on the child's age and the assigned task, as well as if the job repeats daily or weekly, discuss in child-appropriate terms how working produces an earning of something of value. In this case, the child may want to earn stickers, pennies, or an activity outside. Again, the purpose of this activity is not to enslave children to do tasks for you. Rather, the practice teaches your children that a good work ethic helps them earn something they desire.

Setting your children up to be accountable and teaching them that when they work, they earn money, is one of the many basic principles important to success in life. Take the time to teach this valuable life skill when your children are the appropriate age. Remember, start in the playroom.

Catching Them Doing Something Good

Your job as a parent, caregiver, or teacher is to raise well-behaved, conscientious children. When kids misbehave and dislike your redirection, correction, or discipline, tempers are easily lost, and caregivers may become flustered. Try to step back from the situation as if you were at work. Take the emotion out of the situation. Instead, use logic, consequences, and accountability when dealing with poor behavior. To address the situation, say something like, "I know you are upset. However, it is my job as your mother [or father, caregiver, or teacher] to raise you to be safe, honest, caring, self-sufficient, and independent [whatever the situation, use age-appropriate language]. You may not like that I said 'no.' My job is to keep you safe and healthy, and help you learn good behavior. That is my job." Then give the situation some time. Stay calm. You have redirected the behavior or given your opinion or decision on the subject. You have stated that your job is to be the parent and to keep them safe and to steer them onto the straight and narrow path of life.

For small children with short attention spans, redirect the child's attention onto some other positive activity around you: toys, books, outdoor play, etc. Know that there will be meltdowns, tantrums, etc. Children are continually learning to communicate their likes and displeasures. When they are still developing their communication skills, their ability to express disapproval can be difficult, so sometimes they display it through poor behavior. In addition, parents are always learning how to better handle the upsetting behavior. Stay calm, think, redirect the behavior, react logically, and carry on.

To help promote good behavior, always try to "catch [or notice] and compliment" children when they are exhibiting behaviors you want them to continue to portray. This technique is particularly helpful when you are trying to correct poor or dangerous behavior. For example, "I like that you are sitting down and being safe in your highchair." Or "You really shared your toys well with your baby sister this afternoon. Good job. You should feel proud of yourself for being kind." Redirecting the focus of your child's behavior towards the good behavior that you want them to exhibit is easier and more effective for correction than focusing on the negative actions.

Think about the psychology of this method and the outcome of not using redirection. If you always say, "Don't stand up in your highchair ... No, no, no ... no standing. I said, no standing in your highchair. You are going to fall out and get hurt. No, don't do that. No. No. No standing in the highchair," all the child hears, and the immature brain processes, is what not to do ... stand in the highchair. To the toddler, this likely sounds like the suggestion, "Stand in the highchair!"

Look at situations logically. What is good about the bad situation or what is bad about the situation and how can we fix it? When there are issues, do not focus on the word "problem"; rather, change your thinking to a more positive word choice, such as "situation." As author, keynote speaker, and success coach Hal Elrod points out, "We need our brains to be a solution seeking machine, not a problem noticing machine." Acknowledge the situation, and then plan logical solutions. Realize that issues or situations will arise in all children and families. As mentioned near the start of this chapter, for some reason, wherever we find ourselves, we are supposed to be right where we are right now. So, acknowledge the situation, breathe, and then focus on possible solutions.

Age-appropriate discipline will help your child learn to make good decisions later in life. Do not wait until your child is older to teach them good behavior, to teach them how to be kind, helpful, and empathetic. Do the right thing, not the easy thing. Be consistent. Every parent, caregiver, and teacher desires that their children or students like them. That foundational feeling is human nature. However, all caregivers must teach their children to behave so that they can go out in the world, using manners, good behavior, and such, to live more successful and conscientious lives.

My mom used to say, "Little people, little problems. Big people, big problems." There will be situations or problems that arise when your children are little. Provide your children with the skills to handle those little problems or situations when they are young. In doing so, your children will learn to handle big-people problems or situations when they are older. Life is not perfect, but teaching your children how to handle difficult situations from the time they are young helps them handle difficult situations and problems when they are older. Teach empathy, goodness, and being mindful and helpful towards others. If parents fail to teach these positive life skills when children are young, the effects can be devastating to the children later in life.

The following is a real-life example: imagine your daughter's freshman college roommate moves into the dorm, and rather than using half of the drawers in the bathroom vanity, removes all of your daughter's toiletries from the bathroom vanity. The roommate then says that she is taking over the entire vanity and that your daughter should put her toiletries in the other suitemate's bathroom drawers. Your daughter calls home frequently crying because the same other girl says mean, untrue, and condescending statements to your daughter. The same mean roommate, shortly into first semester, decides she will no longer allow your daughter to use her coffee maker and takes all the coffee your daughter purchased. Now you must send your daughter the old Keurig from home via UPS. If you think you are hearing a story from a bad reality show, you are not. This story is true.

It seems the roommate's parents did not do their job as parents. Has this grownup child been set up to be self-sufficient, self-confident, and self-reliable? Unfortunately, she has not.

A teenager does not go off to college and out of nowhere start behaving this poorly. This inappropriate behavior started long before and serves as a cry for help and attention. The unkind roommate is craving attention, whether negative or positive. Who wants to hang out with the hurtful roommate? Likely no one.

Sadly, the unkind roommate stayed in her room by herself when the rest of the dorm enjoyed weekend activities. The roommate began going home on weekends, which further extricated her from joining social circles.

As parents of young children, it is your duty to raise children of character so that they will not grow up like the unhappy, mean roommate mentioned above. Make the world a better place by teaching kindness, sharing, and flexibility from the very beginning of your children's lives. And remember that when you feel your own irritation, disappointment, or impatience flare up, you should pause for a moment and just breathe. Remember, you are where you are, experiencing what you are experiencing right now in the present moment. For some reason, you are here. You are supposed to be going through whatever it is you are going through right now. You will learn from this experience. And this moment, with all of its imperfections, is perfect. Just like you.

We end our chapter with this humorous and poignant excerpt from an unknown author who wrote:

We had a really 'mean' mom ... While other kids ate candy for breakfast, we had to have cereal, eggs, and toast. When others had a Pepsi and a Twinkie for lunch, we had to eat sandwiches. And you can guess our mother fixed us a dinner that was different from what other kids had, too.

Mother insisted on knowing where we were at all times. You'd think we were convicts in a prison. She had to know who our friends were, and what we were doing with them. She insisted that if we said we would be gone for an hour, we would be gone for an hour or less.

We were ashamed to admit, but she had the nerve to break the Child Labor Laws by making us work. We had to wash the dishes, make the beds, learn to cook, vacuum the floor, do laundry, and all sorts of cruel jobs. I think she would lie awake at night thinking of more things for us to do.

She always insisted on us telling the truth, the whole truth, and nothing but the truth. By the time we were teenagers, she could read our minds.

Then, life was really tough. Mother wouldn't let our friends just honk the horn when they drove up. They had to come up to the door so she could meet them.

While everyone else could date when they were 12 or 13, we had to wait until we were 16.

Because of our mother we missed out on lots of things other kids experienced. None of us have ever been caught shoplifting, vandalizing other's property, or ever arrested for any crime. It was all her fault.

Now that we have left home, we are all God-fearing, educated, honest adults. We are doing our best to be mean parents just like Mom was. I think that's what's wrong with the world today. It just doesn't have enough mean moms anymore.

We are given one life, complete with all its imperfections. All families experience challenges. Using grit and grace, you can handle any difficult situation. Take time to breathe and see the light through whatever crisis comes your way. Know that you are right where you are supposed to be right now, and choose to learn from the current situation. In the next lesson, you will find more information to help build your parent confidence and increase your parenting knowledge.

Lesson #3

Build Your Parent Confidence: You Are What You Read, Study, Practice

Life is 10 percent what happens to you and 90 percent how you react to it. — Charles R. Swindoll

Even if everything is as it should be—perfect in its imperfection—no matter how difficult the situation, how do you become an even better parent?

Parents must get their priorities straight if they want to be good examples for their children. Many parents hide in their jobs because they do not know what to do with their kids, how to play with their kids, what to feed their kids, or what to teach their kids. Adults must learn that it is okay that they do not have all the answers. No one knows everything there is to know about raising children. Regardless, parenting comes with great responsibility.

As successful, rewarding parenting results from ongoing learning, it is in the caregiver's best interest to educate themselves any way possible—reading parenting books, listening to parenting podcasts, or observing other families or friends who seem to have good parenting skills and relationships. As written by Mathew Kelly in his book *The Rhythm of Life*: "Surround yourself with people who make you a better version of yourself." Thus, seek out other families, parents, teachers, or caregivers who you feel will help you become better at parenting. Meeting with parent groups through school, church, or online is another way to find other like-minded adults and caregivers who also want to improve their own parenting skills. Friends and families that have similar child-raising goals can provide support for one another during challenging times.

Raising children is an ongoing learning exercise that requires flexibility from parents and caregivers. Be open and transparent while raising kids, and learn to be passionate about becoming a better parent. Build upon your own self-education, improving your personal development so that you are always growing, learning, and expanding your own capacities. To launch you on your own personal development journey, in this chapter, you'll encounter a number of tools for building your self-confidence along with the self-confidence of your child. For example, among other topics, you'll learn about how happiness manifests itself in individuals, the dire effects of comparison syndrome, and the importance of being proactive.

In Pursuit of Happiness

In Dianne Hales' book *An Invitation to Health, Your Life Your Future*, Hales identifies three main factors that contribute to an individual's happiness or well-being, with one of the factors being "Your happiness setpoint—a genetic component that contributes about 50 percent to individual differences in contentment." Essentially, Hales argues that 50 percent of a person's ability to be happy depends on their level of contentment with daily life, which is their "happiness setpoint." This part of life exists when nothing too exciting or too disappointing is occurring. However, each person views life occurrences differently, either positively or negatively. For example, snow on the ground may create grouchiness to a person with an unhappy setpoint, while to an individual with a happy outlook on life, the snowy ground may put a smile on their face and provide them happiness. When you consider a situation that you are dealing with, do you look at the issue with the mindset of the glass-half-full or half-empty mentality? Change your happiness setpoint to focus on the positives, then address the issues. You possess the ability to choose a positive mindset over a negative mindset. So do it!

Hales' second contributing component to happiness and well-being is as follows: "Life circumstances such as income or marital status [...] account for about ten percent." Income only accounts for 10 percent of an individual's overall well-being; intentional decisions can help improve a person's well-being. In 2002, National Academy of Sciences' member, Richard Easterlin stated, "An increase in income, and thus in the goods at one's disposal, does not bring with it a lasting increase in happiness because of the negative effect on utility of hedonic adaptation and social comparison" (2003). In other words, stuff does not equal happiness. In addition to income circumstances, Hales adds, "Having a happy partner may enhance health as much as striving to be happy oneself." Choosing to surround oneself with positive, happy individuals affects both parties' physical and psychological well-being and happiness levels.

Lastly, Hales points out, "Thoughts, behaviors, beliefs, and goal-based activities [...] may account for up to 40 percent of individual variations [in happiness]." An individual's happiness is not limited by their happiness setpoint. Humans innately contain tools to cultivate happiness and import better well-being into their lives. Identifying those tools that help support a positive mental perspective are crucial to maintaining and improving your overall happiness. The science here proves that you have choices and can change your mental happiness outlook, which will ultimately support your self-confidence, which will ultimately allow you to be a better parent or caregiver.

One such tool for increasing your happiness is physical activity and exercise. When practiced regularly, exercise produces happier people. The 2020 research report entitled "The Relationships Between Physical Activity and Life Satisfaction and Happiness among Young, Middle-aged, and Older Adults" states: "A large survey in 24 countries showed that 18–30-year-old young adults with moderate or high physical activity had higher life satisfaction and happiness, and better perceived health. The positive relationship between physical activity and life satisfaction was also found [...] in older adults."

Optimism as well as being mindful also add to a person's levels of happiness and contentment. Mindfulness can be described as proactively and objectively considering thoughts that enter the brain, at the present moment; calmly acknowledging and accepting those thoughts, and then consciously choosing how to react or respond to the thoughts.

Simply said, to increase your level of happiness, you can do the following: get daily exercise, think positively, be mindful, and set goals (more on goal setting later). Each of these important sub-tactics will support your own personal development and self-confidence, thus allowing you to be a better balanced and enlightened parent, caregiver, or teacher.

Understanding the three main happiness factors defined here through science—(1) happiness setpoint, (2) life circumstances, and (3) thoughts, behaviors, beliefs, and goal setting—should help parents, caregivers, and teachers better understand and build their own confidence and well-being. Good parenting confidence results from continual learning, constant practice, shared knowledge, and flexibility, as well as the insight to learn from mistakes. The more knowledge you have as a parent or caregiver, the more confident you will be handling issues involving the children in your care. When adults are confident and well informed on the topics at hand, they will better handle those situations with the children. Children learn best from individuals who have the child's best interest at the forefront of their care. Educating yourself and building your self-confidence through that gained knowledge will better help you guide children through ups and downs, and thus build the children's confidence to better handle situations on their own.

In addition to the information provided, let me remind all adults that by practicing positive "well-being" behaviors, the children within their care will also benefit. Ideally, exhibiting the positive side of behavior and mindset, in front of your children, will result in an increase in happiness setpoint within those children.

Comparison and Contentment Syndrome—Do We Have Enough?

Comparison and contentment syndrome, as well as compulsive comparison disorder, have become commonplace among parents. Do we have enough, do we have enough, do we have enough?

"I am only as good as my neighbor" and "I have got to keep up with what my neighbors have" have become all too familiar sentiments.

Always wanting bigger and better vehicles, bigger and better devices, and for the family ... bigger and better playsets in the yard. Unfortunately, this "keeping up with the Joneses" behavior has become the norm. This compulsive comparison stresses family life and affects relationships. Spending outside of your budget to keep up with the neighbors or other family members can affect finances and create debt. Debt causes stress and is a leading cause of divorce.

Simply said, material items bought on credit literally do not belong to you until you pay off that credit card. The neighbor's expensive European car, your brother-in-law's enormous television and media room, or your best friend's designer handbag are all fantastic items to own if they actually are owned by those people. You have no idea what others' financial situations are; it may be that they have huge credit card payments every month.

Envy and jealousy are ugly and unbecoming. Do you really want enormous amounts of debt just to look good? Is that mentality or reality best for your own dear family?

Focus on your own inner circle, your own family, when it comes to possessions and what you can afford. Many of the wealthiest people in the world drive old cars, reside in moderate homes, and live wonderful, happy lives without striving to keep up with their neighbors. While many parents struggle with the mindset, "I am only as good as my ability to keep up with my neighbors and friends," choose not to participate in that unnecessary battle. Instead, remember: things or material objects are not a sign of success and do not create happiness. Humans, within themselves, create and make their own happiness and have the ability to work, save, and budget for items without breaking the bank.

Strengthen your mind, build your confidence, and focus on your inner circle, meaning those family members whose lives depend on you: your children, spouse, a sibling, a parent. A strong mindset and the ability to focus on what is most important to your family—good health, activities, time spent together, and a strong work ethic; not objects or things—make for a happy and successful family. Kay Wills Wyma's book, *I'm Happy for You (Sort Of ... Not Really)* challenges her readers to choose contentment over comparison and exposes the growing obsession with self-promotion and one-upmanship. Challenge yourself and teach your children through your examples not to place value on objects. Instead, value time spent together where everyone is present and engaged.

A good home life for your family does not mean you have to have every possession that everyone else showcases. Remember, they may not really own them. Men, women, and children are put on this earth to share their own gifts of self and make the world a better place. Excessive materialism has no place in this theory. Starting with children, the world will be a better place if conscientious caregivers raise them to be conscientious as well, instead of focusing on comparing themselves to others.

Observations and Including the Outcast

The dictionary defines the word "observation" as "the action or process of observing something or someone, in order to gain information ... the ability to notice things, especially significant details." Observing children in your care in various settings is an extremely beneficial learning tool for caregivers. Professional education and teaching certifications require many hours of child and student observation for graduation. Simply observing how a child communicates, plays, and interacts with other children will provide the observer with knowledge on how that child interchanges information or ideas. Parents, teachers, and caregivers should continually practice observing the children in their care. When doing so, the parent, teacher, or caregiver can more easily spot irregularities or inconsistencies in behavior and step in as needed to redirect or provide positive solutions when handling behavior situations.

Unbiased observation, meaning simply observing behaviors without "taking sides, placing blame on why a child acts or reacts a certain way, etc." is a learning and documentation tool that every parent and caregiver should utilize when behavioral information is needed to support child behaviors, good or bad, that are brought up at home or school. Practice using this tool to improve your own parenting or teaching skills and, thus, improve your parent, teaching, and/or caregiving confidence.

Surprisingly, formal observations take practice and time. Formal observations must be documented on paper or electronically to include date, location, what occurred, what was said, how children reacted, what adult interaction was conducted, etc. Despite the time and effort, observation, whether formal or informal, is extremely helpful. Caregivers can learn from observations, document improvements in behavior over time, and plan ahead strategies to better assist child interactions. You build your parent and caregiving knowledge and confidence when you take time to observe the children in your care.

Just for fun and if your children are old enough to play alone outside, observe where and what they are playing. Do they tend to gather with neighborhood children at the fancy, colorful swing set or the old one that blends in with the landscape? Remember, you are observing, not comparing. You will likely observe that the children choose to play where there is a feeling of community, imagination, and welcome, rather than what the area or playground looks like. Here is your teachable, "make-the-world-a-better-place" moment. Be the parent or caregiver that creates a positive, safe play zone that welcomes all the children. When the neighborhood children play at your house, you have the added benefit of observation. You will see how the group interacts, as well as see how your child communicates with peers. An additional bonus: you will observe with whom your child plays best.

Teach your children through example to welcome everyone. Of course, if you allow the neighborhood labeled "troublemaker" to play in your yard, the invitation does require that you be even more present so that you can set ground rules and expectations for good behavior. Hosting the neighborhood children involves planning and may make more work for you. However, every moment of play spent in your yard will be worthwhile in the long run. Other neighbors may not agree or may not allow their child to play with the group if the troublemaker is involved, but most won't pay any attention.

Often the neighborhood troublemaker simply hasn't had proper direction from their own parents and just doesn't know how to play. This poor behavior does not mean the child is not loved by their parents. More often than not, poor behavior in a child means that the troublemaker's parents never had proper parenting; perhaps they never had good parenting examples or positive discipline growing up. So how would those parents know how to help their own child with play interactions and behavior when dealing with other children? Why not try to help this broken behavior cycle by welcoming the neighborhood troublemaker to your yard and the play group? Be present, observe, and make sure children are sharing, taking turns, and handling disagreements properly and safely.

You are the adult; this is your yard. You make the yard rules for all the children. Do not play favorites. Use your observation skills. Get involved, and help the kids work out solutions. Remember, children learn by example. Model problem-solving skills. Depending on the age group, get into play mode and act out positive problem-solving skills for all the children involved. Then step out of the play circle and observe how the children handle the problem-solving on their own.

You can teach and children can learn through your examples. Helping others learn to help themselves is known to build self-confidence in the teacher and the learner. If you find that the labeled troublemaker child still cannot play appropriately, try connecting with their parents to develop a solution so that the child can participate appropriately and safely during the next playdate. Invite that child's parents over when the group is playing, so that they too can observe how their child interacts with other children. Observing their own child's inappropriate behavior, amongst children who are behaving age appropriately, may be all that parent needs to set in motion proper discipline and parenting skills. Give these parents the benefit of the doubt, and be kind. You have no idea what their history is or the situations their family may be currently facing. There is no harm in trying to assist your fellow parent. Helping, supporting, and guiding other parents restores faith in humankind, self-confidence in others, and grace all around. Your gut feeling will tell you when to support situations like these, as well as when they are better left to outside professionals such as when group or child safety is an issue.

Never "Buy" Your Kid's Love

This entire chapter was written to provide simple information for building your parenting, teaching, and caregiving confidence so that you can then build confidence in the children you serve. Knowledge is power in that the more one knows about a topic, the more well-rounded that person's bank of information is on the topic. Continual learning and growing from that gained knowledge and experience builds confidence in adults and children.

One oddball topic that all parents, teachers, and caregivers are exposed to but is rarely addressed in parenting material is this one: never "buy" your kid's love. It goes without saying that you should never buy your child things in an attempt to win their love. Instead, to best love your child, show and give them the emotional support they need by being the best parent you can be through your actions and behavior. Be accountable for your actions, follow through with promises you make, and do not promise something you cannot provide. This "being accountable" parental path will do more for the growth and confidence in your child than you think.

As you already know, children get caught up in the "I-want-x-y-and-z-and-I-want-it-now" syndrome. Every family goes through this scenario at some point in life, and usually it starts in grade school. The child comes home and says, "I am the only kid without a blank, blank, blank." As parents, it's hard to say no. For example, your child may say, "Everyone at school has these special erasers" or whatever the latest gimmick or toy of the week might be. Or maybe the dinner conversation starts with, "Joey always wins the Campbell Soup label award every month" or "Mary always sells the most Girl Scout cookies and won the prize again this year because her dad takes the order sheet to his workplace" or "Everyone in my class goes to Disney World. Why can't we go to Disney World?" When these statements come blowing into your home, it might be a good time to consider wisdom from an older generation. My mom always said, "Sometimes life isn't fair."

Your job as parents is to know when to say no and to redirect your child's focus and behavior. Parents, caregivers, and teachers need the skills and confidence to be the parent (or teacher), not the child's best friend. Perhaps your family doesn't use Campbell Soup in their cooking, or maybe selling items that your child is supposed to sell on their own is frowned upon at the office. Explain the concept and the logic here to your child. Know what you can and cannot afford so that you don't ruin a well-thought-out budget just to plan a trip you cannot afford but feel you need to in order to "keep up with the Joneses."

Explain to your child that every family is different and that this difference is okay. Say, "This is the way we run our family. We want you to grow up so that you become independent, self-sufficient, confident, caring, and hardworking, and so you don't just go out and buy everything whenever you want it. We want you to make educated decisions." If the problem continues, give them an honest, verbal example answer that they can use with friends (at their appropriate age level). This strategy takes the pressure off the child for not having or buying the latest gimmick. You might brainstorm with your child ways to handle the situation. Discuss, "What do you think is a good response to say to the child who comments on your x, y, or z issue?" Planning out and practicing communicating responses through role playing helps children with information interaction, builds confidence, and may help reduce any anxiety associated with the situation. Providing response wording for various situations helps children learn to navigate and address these issues by themselves, rather than having nothing to say and then feeling bad about themselves or their situation.

These practices are life lessons that evolve as children grow into adolescents and adults. Addressing issues, brainstorming solutions, as well as providing children with potential answers to challenging questions, needs, and wants in grade school makes it easier to handle as a parent and easier to understand as a child. Starting the practice of verbally addressing these issues and practicing the response will empower your child with communication and coping skills as they grow and move from toddler to preschool, grade school, middle school, high school, and beyond. The verbal saying or mental thought or feeling of "I have to buy my kids x, y, z" or "I have to buy my kid's love" is extremely common, and even more present among single-parent families. Often a single parent feels guilt and wants to buy the child everything to make up for the marital situation or to encourage, subliminally or not, the children to favor them over the other parent. Stop the madness! If you find yourself on either side of this scenario, take a moment to pause. Consider the situation. Is this logical? Is this healthy for you, your child, or the other parent or caregiver? Take a deep breath. Focus. Take the emotion and pain out of the equation. Ask yourself, "What is most important to my child in this situation? Is the toy [or whatever object or activity being debated] really going to help my child or show them that I am the better parent?" Of course not. No. The answer is always, "Right now my child needs to know that they are loved, safe, and that I will always be available to them." No toy or gift can ever replace these three components in a child's life.

In situations where commodities, activities, and trips become the barter system—also known as the "buy-my-child's-love-and-admiration" dialogue between parents, especially in single-parent situations—know that eventually your children figure out what poor behavior you are using to, in a sense, bribe them. This difficult epiphany in your child may not come to fruition until your child is a young adult. However, children will figure out which parent did or did not "do the right thing" when they were young, and this is often a painful realization for them. Consider your child's future mental health if you choose to go the "bribe route" over the "do-the-right-thing" concept. Be strong! You can do it!

Be Proactive

Stephen R. Covey's *The 7 Habits of Highly Effective People* stresses the importance of being proactive first and foremost. Covey writes, "Our behavior is a function of our decisions, not our conditions." Similarly, noted psychologist, Viktor Frankl (who was mentioned earlier in this book) explained that between every stimulus and response, you have the power and the freedom to choose how to react.

When you are faced with a difficult situation, use positive, proactive language, such as, "I will, I can, I prefer, or I'll look at the situation from a different point of view," to help you make sense of it or solve it. Being proactive involves focusing on what you can control, not on factors that are out of your control. For example, you cannot control others' behaviors, reactions, or emotions.

Equally important for proactive people is that they do not blame others for their own mistakes or conditions. Being proactive means acknowledging mistakes, being accountable for the mistake, correcting the mistake, learning from the poor choice made, and then moving on. Proactive humans take daily steps to work toward their goals and strive for ongoing self-improvement and empowerment. As Winston Churchill wisely stated, "Success is not final, failure is not fatal: It is the courage to continue that counts."

On this same theme of being proactive and taking responsibility, Covey also wrote in *The 7 Habits of Highly Effective People*:

Your life doesn't just happen. Whether you're aware of it or not, it's carefully designed by you. You choose happiness or sadness, decisiveness or ambivalence, courage or fear, success, or failure. Being proactive is about persisting in the face of adversity, seeing failures as opportunities to grow, being inspired by the success of others, and continuously working on improving yourself. Remember that every moment, every situation offers you a new choice, giving you the opportunity to do things differently and produce more results.

Build your parenting confidence through continuous learning while striving to be your best self. Sometimes parenting can be difficult, frustrating, and challenging. Other times, parenting is easy. Either way, you have within you all the mental strength you need to learn more and always get better at parenting. Sometimes parent life requires doing your own research, reading more, observing more, listening more, and practicing more patience. Through personal development and practice you will see what capabilities you hold within yourself that are waiting to come out and be applied.

If you still feel less confident than you would like, professional help is always available. Use that inner will and strength that is inherent within yourself, and every human being, and ask for help or recommendations for assistance at your child's school, your church, or your pediatrician's office, etc. Remember, all humans innately want to help others; that gift is called the "hero code" found within all of humanity. So, reach out if you need help. Asking for help and guidance is empowering.

Your self-confidence will flourish with every new resource you secure and study, as well as each new tactic you employ. In turn, your self-confidence is communicated through your behaviors to your children, so that their self-confidence grows as well. Building your child's self-confidence is what we explore in the next chapter.

Lesson #4

Your Child's Confidence

Promise me you'll always remember: you're braver than you believe, stronger than you seem, and smarter than you think! — Winnie-the-Pooh

Without getting too philosophical, humans innately desire happiness. At the end of life, most people look back and remember the good times and regret the bad, no matter who they are, where they come from, or how much money or fame they had during their lifetime. If given their lives to live over again, perhaps they would make different choices, spend more time with family, and do more good in the world. "You must be the change you wish to see in the world," said Mahatma Gandhi.

Basic human life—without all the noise and distraction of the media, social status, the comparison complex, etc.—is about celebrating life. The goal for humans should be to build up those around us, making the world a better place, even if it is simply with a smile. Everyone is special and different in their own way. Children are no exception. Celebrating and acting as people of good character ought to be everyone's life plan.

Children are born full of life. Consider that as a newborn, a child does not know good or bad, right from wrong, confidence or insecurity. All humans are born inherently happy and good and loving. Over time, character traits are formed and instilled in a child through experiences and from their caregivers. So, why do some children exude confidence while others exhibit dependence and insecurity? Many factors, including birth order, child development, and exposure to different types of people and situations form your child's sense of self.

The job of parents, caregivers, and teachers is to do their very best to genuinely and consistently build up their children or students' self-worth through positive reinforcement. Theory tells us that helping others outside of ourselves builds our own self-worth. Equally important is that children see their caregivers building up others around them. Children learn by watching and acting. As a parent, caregiver, or teacher, set a good, authentic example through your own positive behavior and interaction with others. Then watch the amazing transformation in your children as they repeat the positive behaviors that they observed in you, and as their own confidence builds through their supporting others.

Many factors affect confidence in children. In this chapter, we will discuss child confidence as it relates to a variety of related topics, including: learned behavior, handling bullying, "building up" all children, the importance of reading for children, the lifelong benefits of good manners, and supporting your child through their school.

Learned Behaviors

Children learn many of their own behaviors by observing them in others. Some behaviors they learn are good, and teachers, parents, and caregivers are happy when children exhibit those behaviors. At other times, children display negative behaviors. In order to really see your whole child and the range of their behaviors, as already mentioned, it is important to observe them and learn their normal actions and reactions.

As a kindergarten teacher, I had a wonderful five-year-old boy, the oldest of five children, who I realized was cheating. Yes, cheating, in the form of copying, in kindergarten. The situation was baffling and sad at the same time. Cheating in kindergarten made no sense to me. Why would a kindergartener cheat or copy? Why wouldn't the child just ask for help? What inhibited the child's self-confidence to the point that he did not know to ask for help? Where did he learn the concept of cheating, and why did he feel the need to copy?

Timewise, it was the start of the kindergarten school year, so he must have learned the behavior somewhere outside of kindergarten. His behavior suggested that he was insecure about his academic abilities, and possibly his verbal skills, since he didn't engage them to ask for assistance. What I did was nurture the boy, provide him solutions, and reiterate to him that he could ask for help. Doing this eventually helped the boy overcome the cheating tendency. Please notice that to help this boy, I first had to notice the behavior he was exhibiting, the negative behavior, and consistently provide him alternatives without anger or criticism. As an aside, kindergarten, the age of innocence, is not the time to push grades. Kindergarten is a time to learn important life skills, such as asking for help, that will assist children far into adulthood.

Build your child's confidence by teaching them that it is okay to make mistakes and that life is about learning from those mistakes. Most children want to impress their teachers, parents, and families by doing well in school. Do not overemphasize perfection. Celebrate your child's growth, and embrace the fact that your child is doing their best, no matter what level that may be. In addition, if your child appears fearful of making mistakes, do some role playing. Model making a mistake periodically and display, through your actions and voice, the appropriate behaviors to handle and correct the mistake. For example, when you make a mistake in front of your child or classroom, such as spilling some milk, calmly say out loud, "It's okay that I made that mistake. Sometimes, people make mistakes. I can clean up that mess. Next time, I will be more careful at the table [or next time I will take less milk in my glass]."

To an adult, talking through this very, very basic scenario may sound useless. On the contrary, you are providing your child or students a recipe for handling mistakes, mix-ups, and situations that require accountability and action so that they can physically, verbally, and mentally correct future mistakes in a healthy, productive manner. As a child, being able to think through and voice, whether out loud or within, how they are handling a mistake and a challenge is an empowering self-confidence skill that is paramount to future growth.

Bullying

Bullying has occurred since the beginning of time and unfortunately continues to this day. According to the National Center for Education Statistics:

> In 2019, about 22 percent of students aged 12–18 reported being bullied at school during the school year ... Of students in that age range, about 15 percent reported being the subject of rumors; 14 percent reported being made fun of, called names, or insulted; 6 percent reported being excluded from activities on purpose; and 5 percent reported being pushed, shoved, tripped, or spit

on. Additionally, 4 percent of students reported being threatened with harm, and 2 percent each reported that others tried to make them do things they did not want to do and that their property was destroyed by others on purpose.

In the above report, please note that 25 percent of students in the age range were girls, while 19 percent of the students bullied were boys. Sadly, bullying statistics are less often reported in elementary school though bullying is prevalent in the younger grades. You, as a parent, teacher, or caregiver, can change these alarming statistics by teaching and guiding your children while they are still young.

Our responsibility as parents, teachers, and caregivers is to be aware of what is going on in our children's lives from an early age on so that the behaviors can be corrected whether our child is being bullied or bullying others. Equally important is for children, starting when they are young, to recognize when someone else is being bullied and to notify the adult in charge or tell the bully to stop. Child confidence is important here for all involved. Knowing right from wrong empowers a child. A young child or elementary student who is bullied as a kid will likely be bullied later in life and may not be able to handle conflict as a teen and young adult.

Children need to be allowed to identify and express their emotions. Kids of all ages should be taught the importance of voicing their own opinions and oppositions, as well as feel comfortable labeling and sharing what is happening in their lives, both the good and the bad. Often the bullied child feels as though they will get in trouble if they turn in or reprimand the bully. This fearful feeling does not seem logical to adults, but we should realize that this uncomfortable reaction is how the child feels. The more often the child is bullied, the more self-confidence issues build within the bullied child. Unfortunately, that awful, low self-confident feeling and lack of constructive, positive thinking, speaking, or reacting can continue into adolescence and adulthood.

The "mean girl saga" and "boy bullying epidemic" are real problems in today's world. Act as your child's advocate without making the issue worse for your child. Get involved early to find out who your child plays with or hangs out with and who is causing the bullying. In addition, do not assume that your child's teacher is aware of what is happening on the playground or during passing periods throughout your child's school day. Most bullying occurs when a teacher's back is turned, while the child rides on the bus or plays on the playground, while getting a drink at the drinking fountain, or while walking to music class, etc. Regardless of where the incidents occur, schedule a meeting with your child's teacher immediately to discuss the issue and positive solutions. Conceivably, simply changing the seating arrangements in a classroom may solve the issue. Depending on the child's age, perhaps you can plan a playdate for the children and invite the other child's parent/caregiver. Usually, the child who bullies another child was at one time bullied themselves or is currently being bullied and lacks self-confidence. Through bullying others, the bully creates their own self-perceived power and control, as well as a false sense of confidence. Bullying is a vicious cycle that will continue unless the behavior is stopped.

What is crucially imperative if you sense that your child is being bullied? Critically important is that you are aware of your child's normal conduct and emotions. If you notice changes, connect with your child on why they seem sad, angry, extra tired, or sick when they get off the bus or when you pick them up from school. Integral to identifying concerning behaviors is knowing what is normal and abnormal in your child's daily life and behavior. Be observant. If you notice a mood or activity change over time, a recurring sadness, or you have some other concern, your gut feeling is probably correct. There very likely may be something going on.

Document, document, document all bully behaviors, locations, names, dates, and what is said so that you keep a paper trail. Do this documentation electronically and on paper, and then file hard copies in a sturdy file folder. The importance of having bully documentation on paper cannot be stressed enough. Taking copious notes when documenting includes what your child said in quotes and what the others said in quotes (teacher, students, your child, caregiver, etc.), as well as the topics mentioned above. In the unfortunate event that you must meet with school authorities, the amount of on-paper documentation shows thoroughness and research to support your concerns and provides a concrete visualization that equals the amount of pain suffered by your child.

Approach your child's bully situation head-on. Do not wait to act on the situation. Find solutions, not problems. Always respond as your child's advocate while also explaining to them why some children bully other children. Understanding why someone is a bully may help your child be more empathetic as they grow and develop. While there is no excuse for bullying, understanding why kids bully can assist in your child's understanding and may help them create a solution to their own situation. Help your child find ways to express their concerns to their teacher, as well as interact or remove themselves from the bully situation. Always document and involve the teachers and the principal if necessary.

Equally important when dealing with bully situations is to prevent creating a victim mentality in your child. Depending on the brevity of the situation, focus on solutions rather than making your child feel worse by over-discussing and over-focusing on the problem. Focusing on the negative creates a sense of hopelessness in children. Instead, discuss the situation logically and identify solutions, rather than replaying the bad situation over and over.

Remember that you want to help children empower themselves to handle situations on their own (when age-appropriate, of course). Practicing tactics and creating solutions together gives the child a sense of ownership and can help build self-confidence. Some day you, as a parent, caregiver, or teacher, may not be available to step in for the child. Providing children with the strategies and tools to speak up for themselves, seek supervision, and craft solutions will be a confidence builder when solving problems today, as well as in their future.

Build All Children Up, Not Just Your Own

Help your children and students think well of themselves so that they go forth to build and follow their dreams. Provide encouragement, direction, and support. In his book *Winning Every Day*, Lou Holtz addresses this issue by asking the question, "Builder or basher: which are you?" Holtz goes on to say the following:

> Individuals can be divided into two categories: Those who lift you up and those who pull you down. We've all seen spouses who support each other and couples who treat bickering like an Olympic event ... Some parents nurture their child's self-image, others provoke their child's self-loathing. And don't we all know people who never open their mouths unless it is to deprecate something? Feel sorry for those poor souls. They tear

down only to build themselves up. We must teach them by example that the greatest responsibility each of us has is to raise the life condition of everyone we touch. Remember: Encouragement builds success; discouragement breeds contempt. No one can deny the law of cause and effect. Your friends and associates will not think well of you unless you think well of yourself. You cannot think well of yourself unless you think well of others.

The greatest scientists, doctors, astronauts, philosophers, political and business leaders, and even Olympians were once small children who had dreams. In their youth, families, friends, coaches, ministries, and entire communities supported those dreams and encouraged those children to reach amazing goals. That support came in the form of supportive parents, kind teachers, positive coaches, first job bosses, and simple opportunities, as well as challenges, for learning and building the idea that a dream can become reality. Mottos such as, "You can do anything you work hard for and put your mind to" and "You can overcome and persevere. You are valued. You are strong. You will succeed," are the passwords for encouragement that children require to achieve their dreams.

In that same book by Lou Holtz, he writes about the importance of dreaming and hoping. Holtz voices the following:

I've always believed that dreams make the best chauffeurs, because they will drive you anywhere you want to go. Dreamers positively seethe with youthful excitement no matter what their age. I've seen 80-year-olds with teenage eyes sparkling with hope and expectation. They attack each day, foraging every hour for adventure, challenge, and opportunity. Then, sadly there are the 23-year-olds I've seen with eyes as lifeless as tombstones. My guess is that some naysayers have brutalized these young people by denying them their right to dream. We can help them heal by encouraging them to live large lives filled with challenges so that they rise each morning thinking, "Every day someone accomplishes the impossible. Today, that someone will be me!"

My mother once said—and it hurts to hear the phrase as an adult—"Spend time building up your children without spoiling them or creating untruths, because when they go out into the world and grow older, everyone tries to tear them down." That statement was a real bummer to hear straight out of my mother's mouth. Yet, to some, this negative philosophy of living is reality. My mom wasn't recommending that you build up your children superficially, but rather you celebrate their strengths and guide them through challenges. And most importantly, you help children see the wonderful aspects and gifts within themselves—academically, socially, emotionally, spiritually, physically, musically, artistically—whatever gifts the child possesses. When children are genuinely celebrated for their many gifts, they then notice and celebrate natural talents and gifts in others around them, thus building self-confidence in both groups and not succumbing to the negative thinking of others whom they may encounter.

"Everyone has their pluses and minuses" is yet another phrase that my mother continually shares with her grandchildren and children. Perhaps, your mother too has great wisdom in the arena of building child confidence.

Seek out those people who provide you with positive direction. These supportive and valuable resources can be extremely helpful, even if the advice simply comes from experienced family members. Ask for help, advice, and insight when it comes to finding solutions to self-confidence issues in your children. In *Play to Their Strengths*, author Brandon Miller focuses on how adults can help kids see the genius within themselves. He stresses the importance of the "zone of genius." Guide your child, their friends, and those around you to find "their zone." Assist children and help them notice and celebrate their pluses. When age appropriate, help children work on their minuses if you observe the need and the children are so inclined.

Many talents that children possess may be found outside of general school and curriculums; all children and adults have gifts. Good teachers and well-rounded parents will celebrate these strengths in kids and the special aspects related to these traits. Again, modeling authentic support and acknowledgment sets a good example for children and other adults. Practice the previously mentioned very, very simple tactic by noticing and verbalizing out loud words of praise in situations around you. If you see your child's playmate, teacher, or another parent exhibiting a positive behavior, acknowledge that positive action verbally so that your child sees and hears you, and thus learns the positive reinforcement method. Children are more likely to repeat positive behaviors if they see them in others and witness the praise those good behaviors receive.

Supporting All Children at School

As a parent or caregiver, when working or helping at school, equally support your child, as well as all the others in your care. Parents love helping in the classroom, yet sometimes they need to be reminded that they are there to help the entire class, not just their own child. Best practice teaching includes a reminder from the teacher to classroom helpers about the focus of the activity and the directions that they will be assisting with, as well as reiterating that assistants are expected to equally support all children with whom the parent is involved, not just their own child.

The same concept should be reiterated to chaperones who attend field trips. Again, best practice teaching suggests having enough adult chaperones so that the classroom can be divided into small groups. The younger the age of the children, the smaller each group should be. Ideally, the teacher should not lead their own small group. Instead, the teacher, without their own small group, can oversee all groups for educational and safety purposes.

Based on observed experiences, teachers and schools determine very quickly what chaperones are dependable, as well as those who are not and who will not be asked back to help. As a chaperone, do your job, do your best, ask questions, and do not play favorites. Focusing and favoring your child over another sets a poor example for your child and others around you. For safety and security purposes, the chaperone's job is to "have eyes on every child in the group at all times." Be fair and firm.

Research does not show that your child will love you more if you favor them over the other children in your group. Statistics also do not prove that your child will love you less if you do not favor them over the other children. Favoritism is ugly and unprofessional, and most importantly children pick up on the adult's poor behavior from a young age. Don't be "that parent." Children can easily identify the parent who plays favorites.

Believe it or not, your child will learn better behavior and respect you more if you are fair and firm. Fair and firm chaperones get asked back to help at school or on field trips in the future. Chaperones who "play favorites" are not called back. Equally build up all the children in your care and later observe how similar positive behavior is exhibited in the children you lead.

Never Play Favorites

Essentially important is that parents and teachers never play favorites within their own families and classrooms. You can likely name at least five families in your life that had a favorite "prodigal" child. This unhealthy stigma, prolonged within a vicious cycle, occurs and reoccurs from generation to generation. Consider your own family dynamics. Hopefully, favoritism has no place in your home. If you just now are noticing favoritism, stop playing favorites among your children. Focus on each child's gifts and specialties. Spend equal amounts of time with each of your children. Child behavior, both good and bad, is different in every child. Never favor children based on behavior, academics, abilities, etc. No two humans are exactly the same. Even identical twins are not exactly the same and, thus, behave differently and have different interests and different abilities.

When one child is favored over another, lifelong harm and reduced self-esteem result. Children who grow up in favoritism environments learn very quickly who is favored and who is not. Often the result in childhood is that the non-favored child acts out with poor behavior, poor grades, or any behavior that will get attention, despite whether they receive positive or negative attention as a result. The non-favored child simply wants and craves attention, whatever attention or reaction they can get from the adult. Sometimes, the child will do whatever it takes to provoke anger in the adult, just to get some attention. As the child grows, the intensity increases in the poor behavior. This scenario explains the "cry-for-help" behavior in older adolescents, teens, and even adults. Break the cycle, never play favorites. Instead, equally support all children within your care.

Wouldn't the world be a better place if all people, children included, were kind and considerate, as well as supported and congratulated for their veritable traits and behaviors? Teach by example, through your positive, supportive behaviors and voice. Celebrate the pluses, learn from the minuses. Stop the bullying. Never play favorites. And build everyone up.

The Power of Reading

Reading is power. Read, read, and read some more to your children. You cannot over- read to young children or adolescents. Reading impacts both cognitive and affective parts of the brain, as neuroscience reveals. When young readers struggle to develop reading skills as expected, children become discouraged and frustrated, which results in low self-esteem, reduced self-confidence, and increased anxiety. Instead, help build self-confidence in children by reading to them, starting from the time they are infants. Continue reading to them as they begin reading themselves. Know that it is never too late to start reading to your children, no matter their age.

Always choose age-appropriate material when reading to children and students. Get back to your roots and the stories that were read to you. What was your favorite story as a child, and why was that particular book your favorite? Share that story and what you loved about it as a child. Children and students thrive on learning about their parent, teacher, or caregiver's past and thinking about how their parent or teacher lived as a child.

With the hottest new books, be sure to pre-read the story before sharing it with your children or students. Be aware of any hidden agenda within the book, decide if the topic is age appropriate, and then decide whether or not the material should be shared. If you have even the slightest question about the book's quality, integrity, or topic, choose an alternate book. There are thousands of wonderful, well-written, high-quality books written for children on every topic you can imagine. Unfortunately, there also are books that can ruin a child's innocence and be seriously damaging. Choose the right book. Never use a child's book to persuade youngsters or students for or against your personal agenda. Early childhood education and reading materials are no place for topics that are inappropriate, political, or sexual in context, as this material can be detrimental to children.

When toddlers pretend to read in your midst, that darling behavior actually illustrates the beginning of the little one's reading skills. On average, children learn to read between the ages of four and six. However, just because a four-year-old "can read," does not mean that the child understands what they are reading. To test whether a child understands what they are reading, ask questions about the story's content. If the child cannot answer basic questions about what they just read or what the content means, they are not reading for meaning. Reading for meaning is most important. In other words, to be able to read a word but not understand what that word means is not reading for meaning.

The age at which a child begins reading often correlates with when the child began to speak. For example, if your child started talking later than your nephew who is the same age, your child will likely start reading at a later age than your nephew. There is no benefit to learning to read earlier than another child. Learning to read is all about what is developmentally appropriate for your individual child. Just as your child grows at a different rate from another, so too do both children learn to read at different frequencies. Spend time reading with your child, but do not stress if your child begins to read at a slower rate than others. Plenty of late readers excel in school, college, and beyond.

Be sure that while children are learning to read, you always continue reading to them. As they become more and more proficient readers, also continue reading to them. Read together, as well as provide books for your children to peruse on their own. While reading, use your index finger to point to each word. This reading exercise called "one-to-one correspondence" helps children learn that each word makes a sound, has meaning, and when put together, reading each word tells the story. Individually pointing to each word while reading is a skill your child will be taught once they enter school. Introduce this concept at home through your own example and demonstration. This pointing action not only applies to helping your child with reading, but also to mathematics and counting.

Reading actual paper books, over books on a tablet or computer, allows a child the sensory experience of feeling the paper, touching the page, pointing to a word, saying the word, and cataloging that word into memory. Instead of tech or television time, reading books can be a calming experience before naps and bedtime, as well as help develop a child's self-regulation system when it comes to occupying themselves during alone or non-directed times. When toddlers observe adults reading, they learn at an early age that reading is a significant activity in life that can be done for relaxation, pleasure, and learning purposes.

As already mentioned, it is of equal importance that once your child learns to read, you keep reading to them, no matter what their age. Continually reading to your child even after they learn to read themselves provides many benefits: the action of reading to a child, no matter their age, reinforces the importance and love of reading. The vocabulary may be too challenging at that time for the child reader; however, the child learns the story as the caregiver reads, supporting the reading concept and value. The adult reader sets an example for younger readers that reading is a lifelong activity. Exposure to continuous language through reading age-appropriate books expands your child's vocabulary, experiences, problem-solving skills, and adds to the development of self-confidence.

Eventually, children will be able to read the upper-level books that were read to them when they were younger. Hearing the language of books and viewing the pictures from an early age to adolescence develops in the young person a more well-rounded literary sense, increases verbal vocabulary, and fills their brain with knowledge and imagination. A parent, caregiver, or teacher can never read too many age-appropriate books to children.

Practice Manners In and Out of Your Home

Social graces and good manners when taught early in life set your child up for success and ease when communicating with others. Simple social etiquette empowers your child by giving them the social skills to interact with children and adults throughout life, which helps build self-confidence. Teach your children that when they are introduced to adults or a new friend, they should stand up, look the other person in the eye, extend their hand, and say, "Nice to meet you." Through your examples, expect and practice using "please" and "thank you." Kindly remind children or students in your care the appropriate times to use these words. Once your children learn to write, help them write hand-written thank-you notes. Start this practice when your children are young, so that it carries over into adulthood. A wise family member once said, "You never know the power of a thank-you."

Teach your children to open and hold the door for others, as well as kind gestures such as giving up their bus seat to the elderly, to a lady, or to a smaller child. Equally important is for children to practice saying thank you when someone else exhibits these respectful acts towards them.

Myka Meier, etiquette coach, noted author, and founder of the Plaza Hotel Finishing Program, says etiquette makes others feel welcome and shows gratitude. Polite social skills include acknowledging others in a room or at the table, kindness, consideration, and treating others the way you would like to be treated. In a 2020 *Living & Learning* podcast interview, Meier states that the most requests she receives from parents regarding their children is around teaching social skills.

Due to devices, children have less ease with table manners and less confidence in social situations. Unfortunately, children are too often preoccupied with technology. They have lost the ever-important face-to-face interaction skills necessary for discourse, work, and life. From an early age, teach your children to put down toys or devices while at the dinner table. Exemplify, and gently remind children to maintain eye contact while speaking with others. Model taking turns while talking, and redirect them towards appropriate behavior so that children learn that interrupting a speaker is not appropriate. Teaching and expecting these social graces when children are young helps children and students "control the controllable" in social communication situations as they age.

Manners become a habit. To help them take the anxiety out of meeting new people or speaking in front of others, teach children good social manners from the time they are little until they leave the nest.

Support Your Child Through Their School

When your child's school offers family-related activities such as a fun fair, the school play, mother-son brunch, daddy-daughter dance, roller-skating night, the holiday show, family bowling night, etc., take the time to participate with your child and family. You will have fewer and fewer opportunities like these as your children grow up. Spend the time now with your children supporting them, their school, and their teachers. Through your attendance and participation in school or classroom events, you set a good example for your children. The action indicates to your child that their "school world" is important to you and the family; thus, you are supporting your child and helping build their confidence in their learning environments. In addition, these school-sponsored events are a great social option for meeting other parents, as well as your child's classmates and friends.

All About Me

In preschool and early elementary school, teachers often assign an activity to help children learn about each other, introduce public speaking, exercise manners, and build self-confidence. One example might be that each child has a week to be the "Star of the Week" and bring in their "All About Me" poster, which contains a baby photo, as well as photos of family, favorite activities, book, foods, pets, etc. If your child's class offers an activity like this, be sure to participate fully with your child in preparing the materials. This is a fun activity to do together as a family. Additionally, each family member can create their own poster for display at home to include the whole family in the activity.

Some schools allow different daily activities, such as a show-and-tell item, the opportunity to bring in a snack, pet, or favorite stuffed animal during each day for that week's "star" child. The show-and-tell concept is child-centered and should help the child identify the many beneficial interests they have in their life, as well as help them verbalize those aspects of themselves and their families. Think of this activity as the beginning of public speaking for your child. Help and encourage children to feel confident and comfortable speaking about themselves by practicing their presentation at home. These simple activities are another way to celebrate your child or student, while also building their self-confidence.

When considering your student or child's self-confidence, remember that children learn from your example, so be sure that you exhibit good, positive behavior. Just like adults, all children have gifts. Take the time and put forth the effort as a parent, teacher, or caregiver to celebrate those gifts in the children you serve. Build up all children in your care to help develop and support their self-confidence. Watch for signs of bullying. Make reading and good manners a priority in your family or classroom, and then watch how these skills blossom as your children germinate in the garden of life. Making the world a better place by increasing self-confidence in children, one child at a time, will reap benefits for future generations.

Quality parenting, teaching, and caregiving require great amounts of love, discipline, time, effort, and perseverance, yet when the end result is confident, caring, and hardworking children, the position is worth every challenge. No one said parenting or teaching was easy. Parents, teachers, and caregivers get one shot to make a difference in the lives of the children in their care. Be a force for good. As the next chapter reminds us, always, always show up and advocate for your children and students.

Lesson #5

Advocate for Your Child: You Get One Chance. Show Up

If your actions inspire others to dream more, learn more, do more and become more, you are a leader. — John Quincy Adams

In Latin, the root of the word "parenting" means "to bring forth potential." Advocating for your child from an early age requires you to offer total support and warmth, as well as guide, teach, and expect good choices in your child. Wise parenting, caregiving, and teaching bring forth potential in children and require that adults act as counsel for them in areas inside and outside of the home. All parents want to protect their children from harm, mistreatment, and failure. Psychologically wise and involved parents guide their children, advocating for them along the way, without hindering the development of their independence through overprotection. As a parent, caregiver, or teacher, you get one chance to be a mentor to the children in your care; show up with grace, firmly support them, and be an advocate for good in their lives. Parents: channel, direct, and, thus, "bring forth" your child's potential.

This chapter covers a wide variety of topics that require your consideration as they can have negative effects on your child if you fail to educate yourself and neglect advocating on your child's behalf. I have split the chapter into five sections to include the following themes: school selection, learning from your child and through parent-teacher conferences, school educational materials, extracurriculars, sleep and nutrition, and caregivers.

School: Choosing the Right School for Your Child

Fear stems from not knowing a lot about a topic. Some say that the letters in the word "fear" stand for "False Evidence Appearing Real," which can cause anxiety, procrastination, or avoidance of a situation that may or may not come to fruition. Usually, the fear stems from the subconscious thought that you will not be able to handle the situation, rather than the reality of the situation. I bring this up because when it comes to choosing your children's school, many parents simply become overwhelmed and afraid. The cure? Be proactive! Do your research when selecting the school that is right for your child. Knowledge is power and sets a parent/caregiver up with the information needed to address situations and make decisions without anxiety. The following are several common school options.

Public, private, charter, Montessori, and Waldorf schooling methods are just a few of the many educational options available to families. Every child learns differently. Various education methods and theories work for different learning characteristics and styles in children. The following descriptions of each may seem like common knowledge, but knowing your options, as well as the pluses and minuses of education types, empowers you to make better informed decisions when it comes to your specific child's education. Some of these educational school types and methodologies may not be available in your area. Even still, it's helpful to be informed about the options out there.

Public school typically starts in kindergarten, finishes in 12th grade, and usually offers additional services for students in need of speech therapy, occupational therapy, English as a second language (ESL), individual education programs (IEP), special needs teaching, paraprofessional classroom aids, and such. Public schooling and most extra services provided within a school district are free to residents and paid for through your property taxes.

Private schools are paid for out of pocket and may be connected to a church, parish, synagogue, etc., or related to a specific type of learning, such as foreign languages or specific education models such as Montessori or Waldorf.

Montessori education, as defined by the National Center for Montessori in the Public Sector, is named after its founder, an Italian scientist, medical doctor, and educator, Maria Montessori. First developed in 1907, Montessori is practiced in public and private schools around the world, educating children from birth to age 18. Based on the founder's scientific observation of human development, the Montessori model recognizes birth to age six as an intense period of formative development with cognitive, social, and emotional outcomes. Students in mixed age groups choose their own work and work at their own pace while Montessori-trained teachers present a comprehensive curriculum individualized for each child. Montessori learning materials are hands-on and designed to engage curiosity, independence, and self-guided learning. The traditional Montessori method of education does not include any pretend or imaginary play, such as pretending to be a fairy, dragon, etc. Instead, traditional early childhood Montessori play is based on utilitarian practices such as washing dishes, building a house, or creating actual figures in society or history; for example, dressing up like Abraham Lincoln to learn more about him. To further explain, orthodox Montessori practices typically would not include, for example, the concept of a leprechaun for St. Patrick's Day, or they may say there is no such thing as Santa Claus when teaching cultural holidays of the world-type topics. I am not saying this is good or bad; rather I'm providing information so that you, as parents, can make educated decisions for your specific child.

In comparison, the Waldorf education method offers developmentally appropriate, experiential, and academically rigorous educational topics while integrating the arts in all academic disciplines for children in preschool through 12th grade. Waldorf education is based on the insights, teachings, and principles of early 20th century artist and scientist, Rudolf Steiner. The method's principles evolved from an understanding of human development, as well as the needs of the growing child. Music, dance, theater, writing, literature, legends, and myths are not simply subjects to be read about and get tested on. Instead, Waldorf students physically experience each subject, further cultivating their intellectual, emotional, physical, and spiritual capacities. The Waldorf theory suggests that experiencing academics through the arts helps students learn more distinctly, so they can set a future path for themselves and act in service to the world.

Based on your own child's abilities and needs, choose the best fit school type for your child. Pay attention when choosing schools so that you stay within your family's budget. Never select a school based on popularity, what friends are selecting, or what school is "hot" in current social circles. School selection is extremely important as your child will begin to spend more time at school than at home. Elementary school is essential to every child's life, leaves lasting impressions, helps to form educational foundations, and prepares them for their future. Choose wisely the school that you believe your child will feel most comfortable attending, as well as thrive in educationally and socially.

Homeschool vs. Traditional School

Which type of schooling—homeschool or traditional—works best for your child and your family? There are benefits to homeschooling, as well as obtaining a public or private education through traditional schooling methods. As a result of the 2020 pandemic, many families turned to homeschooling because they were not happy with the online teaching provided by schools. Different school methods work for different learners. As with any profession, some parents thrive as homeschool teachers, while others know that teaching is not in their wheelhouse. Be honest with yourself, and acknowledge your capabilities and areas of insufficiency with regard to homeschooling. Research your education options. The following two paragraphs offer a brief explanation to help you better understand homeschooling:

Public Charter Homeschool Programs work with homeschooling families to provide public school learning materials and curriculum that can be done at home. Homeschool programs and accreditation vary by state but still offer the "conveyor belt subjects" of mainstream education. Some districts even provide services such as speech, occupational therapy, inclusion in sports, etc., to homeschooled students. Many children thrive better socially, emotionally, and academically in homeschool programs. The smaller class sizes, lack of peer pressure, lack of bullying, and more directed teaching allows them to discover extra passions and gifts in their own learning style. Homeschooling in older children is more common for students such as athletes with rigorous training, travel, and competition schedules that conflict with normal school hours.

Homeschool programs must file and provide documentation to local school districts or the state to ensure that students meet the typical education benchmarks. Prior to your children reaching high school levels, be sure your child's homeschool program will be accepted by their potential high school, as well as universities and colleges, especially if higher education is desired. Be aware that not all homeschool programs are accepted by high schools or colleges, so do your research before you enroll your child in any nontraditional schooling.

Whenever possible, choose in-person schooling or homeschooling over online schooling (more on this later in this chapter). The benefit of in-person instruction inside a real classroom is teacher accountability and student accountability, as well as the extremely important development and finetuning of student social skills. In a well-run school, the principal or assistant principal makes daily rounds, checking in on classes and teachers' instruction. Yearly observations for annual reviews are done to validate good teachers and identify and provide support to those who are struggling. Great schools with great teachers are typically led by great principals.

To help you select the right school for your child and get a feel for the school's atmosphere, do your own research on the district, school, and principal. When my family was looking at schools, I knew the local public elementary principal was well liked and interacted positively with teachers and students because I observed those behaviors on my pre-visit to the school. Before sending my children there, I scheduled a meeting with the school because I wanted to learn more about the school, the teachers, and the curriculum to determine if the environment would be welcoming and a good fit for my children.

While walking through the halls, the children always said hello and interacted with my tour guide, the principal. This well-liked leader helped create a happy, positive environment for students. He visited classrooms, walked through the lunchroom, and was present in the morning and afternoon when students arrived and departed. The principal and assistant principal also made an effort to take a stroll around the playground during recess to "be present" for the students. The daily playground visits allowed the principal to watch the various interactions between teachers and students, thus holding all accountable while letting everyone know he was approachable, which comes in handy when issues arise. If you make an effort to visit potential school options, and you don't have a good feeling when a visit concludes, perhaps that school isn't the right fit for your child.

Talking With Your Child and Their Teachers

Once you have selected the best school and learning environment for your child, take time daily to listen and learn about their school day. "Out of the mouths of babes" comes truth. Attentively listen to the stories and anecdotes your child shares regarding their school day. Young children typically do not lie. Born without that quality, lying and dishonesty are learned behaviors often developed out of fear. When your child returns from school or during the ride home, ask questions about their school day. If your child attends preschool, often that day's topics and activities are displayed for parents. Asking questions about the posted daily schedule helps a child expand on their day.

Remember, do not ask close-ended questions that can be answered with yes or no replies. If your child is tired or not in the mood for dialogue, table the discussion and questions for later. Another avenue for learning about your child, their academics, and their school is parent-teacher conferences.

Once you have selected and enrolled your child in school, make an effort to engage in the school's many offerings. In-person conferences, usually held twice a year, not only allow you to hear about how your child is doing in school but also help build a relationship between you and your child's teacher, as well as give you a sense of your child's school day. Parents must make the conscious commitment to attend their child's parent-teacher conferences with confidence, open-mindedness, willingness to learn, and mutual respect for teachers. A good teacher will be respectful of you and your concerns, as well as your child and their various learning styles. The best teachers are always willing to adjust, learn, and improve their teaching and communication skills.

Several years after I taught a young first grader, I ran into the child's mother. The parent filled me in on "all things Michael." She reminded me that at a previous parent-teacher conference for her son, I had mentioned that Michael did not color in the lines. She thought that was funny. My observations obviously bothered her since she brought it up years later. At the time of the conference, I explained the activity and that the lesson had two goals: teaching an academic concept, as well as learning to take ownership in doing your best work, no matter the project or assignment. This premise had been the objective of the assignment for all the students. Obviously, as a teacher meeting for yearly conferences, I did not get that point across clearly to this parent because they brought it to my attention years later. At conference time, I meant no harm or disrespect. I was merely pointing out the normal developmental maturity/immaturity in the student at that time, as well as the concept of learning the value of creating good, quality work. Clearly, I needed to do a better job explaining to the parents the normal immaturity and the reasons why doing work at any level is always a stepping stone for future learning.

Before attending your parent-teacher conference, choose to be positive and open to recommendations. Handle the meeting with grace even if there are difficult issues discussed or personality conflicts between you and the school staff. Rise up and choose inspiration when learning from the teachers' suggestions. Engage their help and expertise. Most teachers chose education as their profession because they love working with children and want to help students learn to the best of each child's ability.

Here is an example of what happens when parents fail to interact with their child's teacher and school: John attended a Montessori preschool for two years. Then he became a kindergarten student in my class. When he came to his kindergarten conference at the start of school, his parents mentioned to me that just two weeks before his Montessori preschool ended, they were told, "John has misbehaved his entire time at school, he is behind academically, and he never completes his work." The parents were shocked that the school waited that long, an entire school year, to inform them about their child's development and poor behavior. This result is not solely the preschool's fault, and not solely due to the type of preschool—Montessori. If, earlier in the school year, the parents had been proactive, sought out their child's teachers, learned the school's methodologies, mission, and focus, and checked in on how their child was doing during conferences and at other times, the parents would have had an idea about their son's ongoing difficulties in class. Equally important, the teachers should have requested a meeting with the parents at the start of the school year when the behavior began.

Back to conferences—when attending conferences, bring a list of questions for the teacher. Besides the general academic questions and depending on the child's age, ask how your student behaves socially and emotionally. Try to refrain from questions that can be answered with a simple yes or no response. Always ask the teacher to elaborate on their answers so that you receive solid feedback and valuable information about your child. Some sample questions might include: what are my child's strengths in the classroom and academically? In what areas do they need continued practice? How does my child interact with others? Who does my child play with most? Does my child appear to make friends and interact easily? What does my child do on the playground?

Playground interaction is an area that I have found to be most neglected in the education field. Schools supply the playground and monitors, but they do not provide play support to the students. As a teacher, I often observed children who did not have someone to play with, who did not know how to interact or enter into an existing playground group, or who were bullied out of the play group and left to play by themselves. The observation was heartbreaking as a teacher, as well as a parent.

Years after retiring from teaching, I noticed this exclusion behavior towards my own child when she was in kindergarten. At the time and to this day, based on my teaching experience and observations, I believe that there is a great need for teaching these crucial playground social skills. Unfortunately, increased screen usage (on tablets, phones, and computers) as a means of baby-sitting or keeping a child occupied has drastically affected social skills, behavior, and problem resolution development in many children. These social interaction skills should be taught at home from a young age on and at school, ideally starting in preschool.

For the betterment of all children and society, every school should take the initiative to involve parent volunteers or school employees to observe playground behaviors, then take steps to teach children and encourage the inclusion of any child being left out and ostracized. Playground play specialists and monitors could gather the multiple children who are being left out, each playing by themselves, and create their own social play circle of friends. Wouldn't it be great if those excluded children could get together and create their own group? In young children, this concept needs to be modeled by an adult so that the students learn as they grow older to practice including others, rather than excluding.

While at conferences, ask about your child's playground interaction. If enough parents ask, more attention and observation will be done to improve playground social skills.

During your parent-teacher conference, if your child's teacher recommends outside help, academically or socially, such as a therapist, learning resource teacher, tutor, etc., consider what documentation the teacher has taken on your child academically, as well as notes taken on your child's behavior, that warrant seeking help inside or outside of school. Do not feel badly if your child needs additional help. Be grateful that a teacher has brought this concern to your attention. Great teachers want to help all children, especially those who require extra support. Think of this as an opportunity for growth in your child and yourself. You were put on this earth to be a parent, and here is your chance to learn more and help your child succeed. Ask, "What can we do at home to help? What are you doing in class as a teacher to assist my child with this issue?" Perhaps moving the child's seat location will reduce distractions for the child. Be open to the teacher's suggestions.

Equally important is conducting your own non-biased observations, as well as possibly obtaining another analysis of your child from your own professional sources. Ask if you can help in your child's classroom (once or on a weekly or monthly basis) and possibly observe the behaviors that the teacher is noticing.

Teachers often implement sticker programs and charts to help promote good behavior in young children. Stickers are added to a chart at the child's desk when good behavior is observed. Some teachers use gimmicks such as the old "red, yellow, and green traffic light" charts displayed on the board identifying good behavior (green); whoa, check that behavior (yellow); and stop the bad behavior (red) columns. All student names start the day in the green column. When a child displays poor behavior, their name is written in the traffic light column according to the behavior. The hope, while using this concept, is that as the child progresses from poor (red) behavior, their name will be moved over to the columns that identify improving behavior (yellow) or back to good behavior (green). These charts can work well or not, depending on the accountability of the teacher and the time frames measured and rewarded.

Little kids work best with short time frames. Remember, some social situations and sitting for long periods of time often make it hard to "be good" for long periods of time. For the developmentally immature, it is very difficult to be good all day. This is very normal. Consider the behavior modification chart concept, as well as the time frame being observed. Teachers should break up the time frame into short amounts of time or for each subject or activity.

Some children thrive on behavior sticker charts while for other children, the activity does not produce positive results. Children should never be punished for lack of stickers on a chart or having their name written on the traffic light board all day. Unfortunately, for the children whom the sticker chart or traffic light does not work, those children never experience success and perceive that they themselves are not good. If the behavior charts result in a prize and your child comes home saying, "I never get to pick a prize from the treasure box," either due to poor behavior or when a teacher forgets, that outcome is extremely discouraging for children of any age. My personal teaching opinion is that redirecting inappropriate behavior and praising appropriate behavior is far more effective and efficient, and less damaging to student self-confidence in the classroom than prizes, etc.

While attending your parent-teacher visit, do not overstay your conference time. Remember, on conference day, teachers are only allowed a few minutes to meet with each student's parents or caregiver. Often, teachers meet with as many as 60 parents individually, depending on the conference layout. Consider your teacher's day of conferences, and plan your visit accordingly. If you need more time with your child's teacher, while you are there, schedule a meeting for a later date. Make a note to reconnect after the conference to gauge your child's progress or further discuss different points.

Following parent-teacher conferences and other school visits, take some time to tell your child about your visit. Don't forget to let your child know how much you enjoyed seeing the classroom and hearing all the wonderful comments the teacher made about them. Always, always discuss and praise the good behaviors that were mentioned and celebrate them. Graciously address with your child their teacher's concerns or the behavior that needs work. Using an open dialogue, discuss areas that the teacher mentioned need attention. Never blame outside forces for areas of concern. Listen to your child's side of the story. Take time together to plan steps to help your child in the areas that they need assistance and support. Be proactive. Obtain documentation and information and be open to learning more from your child's teacher; engage their help and expertise.

In addition, following parent-teacher conferences or other meetings involving your child, always write a quick thank-you note when you get home. Do it immediately while the conference topics are fresh in your mind. A put-off thank-you note rarely gets written. An important note here, many parents never take the time to thank teachers. As a parent or caregiver of young children, remember, your child will be in school for many years. Creating a positive, open relationship with your child's school and teachers will make each visit feel less daunting and more enjoyable, which is the ideal for which parents and teachers strive.

Did you know that more often than not, schools and teachers are told what is not working, focusing on negative issues? At conferences and in the thank-you note, find something good to thank the teacher for; then work together to find solutions to issues that are not going well. Remember, teachers, children, and parents are human. Make a concerted effort to build each other up, rather than tear each other down. Do the right thing and your day will be better, your child's day will be better, and you will have done your part to make the world a better place, one small thank-you note at a time.

As your child grows and moves into higher grades, continue to attend their conferences, even into high school and even if the teacher says you do not need a conference. Schedule one anyway. A conference holds the teacher accountable for reporting on your child, continues relationship building between parent and teacher, shows support for your child, and keeps the lines of communication open between both parties. These brief meetings open the door for future interactions. Being comfortable with your child's teacher is extremely helpful if later a problem arises at school. Get into the habit of attending conferences held twice a year. You will learn valuable information about your child, your child's teacher, and your child's school.

Following your child's conference, especially if what you learned about your child was unexpected or stressful, always remind yourself that all children are special in their very own ways. Every child is unique and learns uniquely as well. Katrina Kenison's books *The Gift of an Ordinary Day* and *Mitten Strings for God* share the author's motherly insight on identifying and celebrating differences in children, even when those differences produce challenges. Her books are yet another resource reminding parents to focus on their own children and to stay away from comparing their children to other children outside the family. This message is especially pertinent when your children enter preschool and elementary school. In today's tumultuous world, new parents may find this concept difficult due to social circles, as well as social media and the pressures that undoubtedly result. Stay true to your roots, to the gut feeling you have as a parent when considering your child's growth academically, behaviorally, and socially.

When addressing school academics and behaviors brought to your attention at conferences or throughout the school year, think back to the basics that you grew up with or your parents taught you. Hopefully you experienced positive parenting. If not, acknowledge that, and change your own family's history by learning all you can to become your best parenting self. Do your research so that you can make wise, educated, and logical decisions and choices that work for you and your children.

Family and parent life will be far more rewarding if you spend time noticing and supporting your own children's gifts and your own family's pluses. Do not fall into the parent popularity crowd at school, the neighborhood, ballet class, or the ballpark. Always remember that your child's education and growth do not coincide with popularity as a parent. Support your children and their education to the best of your ability by focusing on the most appropriate schooling, whatever that may be, as well as fostering communication lines with teachers.

School Curriculum: What Are They Teaching My Child?

Historically speaking, unless you were in the education field, parents simply assumed and trusted that school districts taught the same basic academic subjects that they were taught growing up: math, English, science, social studies, history, etc. Curriculum, defined as the subjects comprising a course of study in a school, was once carefully chosen by the school district to include those traditional learning subjects that were paramount to a child's education. Teachers then disseminated the information in the classroom without pushing any agendas, and inappropriate behavior by teachers was strictly frowned upon and not allowed.

Unfortunately, today, many districts and educators have forgotten about the ethical purpose of teaching—to build and provide truthful information to students, so they can go forth and make educated, logical decisions based on historically correct fact, as well as conduct productive interactive discourse with others for the civilized exchange of information. Shockingly, the basic subject content taught at many schools has morphed into unrecognizable material in critical subjects including science, history, social studies, etc. The content distortion has become so widespread from early childhood to post college levels that history, just one example, is literally being changed and rewritten containing historical mistruths.

So, I ask you—have you thoroughly checked out the school and district where you plan to send your child? What subjects and topics are being taught at the school? What materials are used for teaching? Are personal, inappropriate agendas being woven into classes? Pay very close attention. Education has changed substantially since you were a student. Ask questions, and request to see a copy of the various curriculum. Education is extremely different than it was just ten years ago. Your tax dollars pay your local school's budget, administrators and teachers' salaries, and learning material purchases. You have a right to know what types of curriculums are being taught at your child's current school.

Besides just the learning materials at your child's school or potential school, what values do you see being taught, modeled, and expected for students? Are they values you support within your family? Do they promote goodness, kindness, building up society, or tearing it down? Condoleezza Rice, the 66th U.S. Secretary of State, stated in a conversation on April 28, 2022, "Too many of our great institutions are afraid to talk about values anymore for fear of offending somebody. I don't have to offend you by acknowledging my values. I want you to acknowledge yours too ... but none of us is helped by being silent about our values and pretending that they aren't important. That's what gets countries and people and democracies and societies into trouble ... when they're afraid to recognize that human beings are driven by more than just a set of observable needs. There's something 'in here [pointing to her heart],' that has to be right."

To learn more about what is being taught in your school and district, attend the school's PTO/PIC (parent teacher organization/parent information committee) meetings and/or the district board meetings held monthly. Every school offers these types of organizations. They may be titled differently depending on the school. Attending monthly parent information meetings will give you a glimpse into the school's focus, issues, pluses, and minuses. In addition, you may learn what "hot button" issues have staff or parents concerned. You need to be aware of and knowledgeable on topics affecting your child and your family, so make a concerted effort to stay informed through these informational sessions. If you are unable to attend the meetings every month, at minimum attend the first meeting of the school year. In-person meeting attendance is always a better choice for accountability purposes; however, if you experience scheduling conflicts, some school districts now offer these meetings via video conference.

Understand current buzzwords and controversial topics affecting school districts, and, thus, your child. Educate yourself. Know your rights. Maintain your own family's values by choosing schools in districts that support those values.

With regard to remote learning situations, pay attention to online teachers and the material being taught. Be seen in the background of your child's online class without being distracting. You are the parent, and it is your right to know what your child is being taught. That said, no parent should interact with the teacher or student while the child and other students are in an online classroom session. Imagine that behavior in an actual in-person class. Not appropriate.

The point here is to be present to what is being taught and how it is being taught in the classroom and online. Are the learning materials appropriate and in line with your family values? Do the learning materials and instruction actually relate to the subject of the class? Is the teacher teaching the subject identified for that class or something different? I have observed a live online professor teaching a childhood literature class ask students to watch the presidential inauguration of that professor's political party for extra credit. Again, it was completely inappropriate as the assignment does not relate to childhood literature. In the next live online class period, the professor asked students whether or not they had watched the inauguration. The childhood literature class was held via Zoom, so all students were required to be visible and provide their answers. Next, the professor told the class if they had not watched the live inauguration, she would give students another chance; if they watched the replay of the inauguration, students could still receive extra credit. If the class had been a political science class, the assignment would be a natural fit. Remember, it was a childhood literature class.

This inappropriate behavior is a perfect example of a professor pushing their own political agenda during an online class, with zero ties to the course topic, while most parents were not paying attention. The sad part of stories like this is that the students are too afraid to speak up for fear of poor grades. What is more disheartening is that this problem exists nationwide from post college levels all the way down to preschool. You must stay informed as parents, caregivers, and teachers, so you know what your child is being taught, starting in preschool through college.

To further document the point that you should be aware of what your children are learning, here is another shocking example. I know middle school children who were given a school day off if they attended a protest at the town's local courthouse in support of the teacher's agenda. This teacher- and school-supported activity was not in the best interest of student learning. Consider the educational time lost for those students when not attending school for an entire day, let alone the inappropriate shaming of the students who were not allowed to attend the protest because their parents wanted their children in school. These two examples are the tip of the iceberg, you might say, when it comes to agendas being pushed at some schools. My point, pay attention to what and how your children are taught. What are your children learning, and is that material in alignment with your family values?

Extracurricular Activities: Don't Over Program

Another area that you, as a parent, will find requires advocating on behalf of your child is extracurricular activities. Once your child begins participating in extracurricular activities, such as art, music, dance, sports, Daisy Scouts, Cub Scouts, etc., take the time to observe your child. Are they enjoying the group, instructor or coach, and the activity? Do they interact with the other children? No one knows when a child is four years old if they will be a famous artist as an adult. Children do not have to be Picassos at age 4. If art class was a disaster, the child may never do another art class. Or, just maybe the disastrous class sparked positive interactions and learning that will spill over into a different activity for the child.

Children are continuously learning. Humans never stop learning. Once your child begins participating in extracurriculars, discuss the activities with your child. What did they learn? What did they like or dislike? Would they like to attend again? Be open to the positive and negative reactions and learn from them. If this activity was not what you or your child expected, don't stress. There are a million opportunities waiting to be discovered by you and your child. Do not rule out trying something new that your child thinks they would like if this activity did not turn out to be a favorite.

Whether you are already knee deep in early childhood activities, classes, sports, and playgroups, or just beginning the search for your child's first activity, consider the following to help make the best-educated decisions as they pertain to your child and family.

Most important—don't over program with too many activities. Choose one to try at a time, especially when children are very young.

Variety is important. Participating in school and non-school activities, clubs, and sports allows children, as they get older, to meet and interact with different student groups. This offers them diversity from the daily interactions they have at school.

Always follow through. If you and your child sign up to attend an activity, follow through and participate. Be accountable and set a good example for your child and others. As previously mentioned, never sign up for an activity you cannot or will not attend. Doing so teaches your child that it's okay to be unreliable and unaccountable. Remember, children are always watching you. Do you want your child to copy your poor behavior and carry that negative reputation through life? Of course not! Follow through with the activity you told your child you both would attend. Go to practices, participate fully, and at the end of the session if your child or you do not want to continue that particular extracurricular activity, don't sign up for the next session. It's okay if the activity didn't turn out the way you had hoped. Consider different options, and try something new.

Encourage! Don't discourage. I've actually heard parents say to children the following heartbreaking comments: "You're not going to play in the game tonight, so we don't have to go to practice." Another parent commented, "You're not as good as your cousin, so we aren't going to swim today." No child ever deserves to be spoken to like this. Language insinuating failure, even if it is spoken in a matter-of-fact tone, sets the child up to quit even before giving an activity a chance. Repeated comments such as these cause low self-esteem and instill a false sense of low worth and lack of ability and purpose in any individual.

Stay in your budget. Don't sign up for something you cannot afford just because your best friend is signing up their child. Refer back to the dangers of the "keeping-up-with-the-Joneses" mentality. Focus on what is best for your family. Strong family values, including the wallet, need to be considered. This recommendation applies when your child is a toddler all the way through to the day that they leave the nest and are no longer under your financial care.

Choose the best instructors for your specific child. This point comes more into play once your child is in elementary school and beyond. However, if a child has zeroed in on a particular sport early, caregivers can be on the lookout for future coaches. Selection should not be solely based on an instructor's past successes. Look beyond those accomplishments to the type of coach that will be interacting with your child. If you take the time to observe the plethora of coaches available in the activity your child finds most enjoyable, those observations will help you choose a best-fit coach. Consider the following when observing and selecting instructors and coaches:

- Watch how they interact with children (others and your own).

- Observe if they show up on time.

- Determine if they are accountable for what they say they will do.

- Notice if they expect kids to work hard and do their best (age-appropriately of course).

- Determine if they build up your young child.

- Take note whether they provide positive reinforcement or negative feedback when mistakes are made.

- Be aware of how respectful of time they are, both with your child and the next child's lesson.

You should know when it is time to upgrade coaches for the next level of your child's involvement. Do what you feel is best for your child, not for you. Remember, you are the parent, not the child participating.

Consider when it is time to change activities and understand that your child may not enjoy the same extracurriculars you did as a child. And that is okay. The purpose of participation in sports, music classes, art classes, cooking classes, Scouts, etc., at an early age is to help develop the whole child and potentially identify some activities your child loves. Diversity is key. Remember, all experiences, good and bad, add to the formation of the adolescent that your child grows into and becomes. You, as the parent, are gifted with the opportunity to help mold that individual. That being said, you cannot force any individual, in this case your child, into being something they are not meant to be. Like you and I, children grow up good at some things and not so good at others. We may like basketball, but they do not. Remember, these differences make children and us who we are and add to our individual uniqueness, and that is okay!

Again, be grateful for the opportunity to enroll your child in various activities. Handle with grace the ups and downs of their learning and your juggling to get them to those activities.

Nutrition and Sleep

Advocating for your children typically means managing what's going on outside of your home. However, it is equally important to support your children and family from inside your home. Balanced nutrition and adequate sleep are foundations for a healthy childhood. Consider your child's diet. Nutrition is a parenting area in which you have control. Proper healthy nutrition is pivotal to growth in young children, adolescents, and adults. Start early helping children make good food choices by providing and eating healthy, wholesome foods in your home and at restaurants. Feeding children for longevity supports the development of their brain, heart, muscles, bones, and entire body. In addition, healthy foods help foster good mental health in children. Good nutrition helps prevent illness, as well as reduces the effects and duration of any sickness.

Eating for energy and good health is not expensive, but it does take some time, thought, and planning. Your family's diet should come from foods sourced directly from nature such as fresh fruits, vegetables, greens, non-processed high-fiber whole grains, cereals, and breads (stay away from white breads, white rice, and white pastas), lean meats, fish, and eggs. Studies prove that the two main factors that result in low energy and fatigue are poor nutrition and chronic stress. You have control over what foods you feed your family. Choose foods wisely; take care of yourself and your children by eating wholesome, nutritious foods.

Providing your children with healthy meals and snacks, without denying them the occasional treat, is important for their overall development. Do your best to prevent children from consuming too much sugar, processed foods, and sugary drinks. When children are taught about and served healthy foods from an early age, often the result is that those children choose healthier foods as they grow into teens and young adults.

Equally important to nutrition is adequate sleep. Your child's health, growth, and overall well-being depend on a good night's sleep, and naps, especially for younger children. To ensure that your child sleeps long enough and gets their required rest, set consistent sleep schedules and routines, and use the evening as a time to help them slowly quiet down after their day. A relaxing bath and story are a good way to wind down at any age. Bedtime routines and adequate sleep are even more important with school-age children as a good night's rest better prepares them to handle the educational day. You know your child and how much sleep they need in order for them to wake up happy and well rested. Exact hours vary from child to child, so if you have concerns about your child's sleepless nights or poor sleep habits, talk to your pediatrician.

Daycare and Sitters

Parenting and caregiving are noble professions that require great amounts of time, energy, love, and support. Equally important is that you maintain your own selfcare, both mentally and physically, as an individual and as parenting, caregiving, or teaching partners. The importance of taking time with your significant other cannot be understated. However, date night does require a babysitter for young children while you are away. Who will you choose?

In addition, if both adults in your household work away from home, you may be required to hire daycare providers outside or inside your home. Be sure to thoroughly vet your babysitters before you hire them. Ask friends for their recommendations for babysitters and daycare providers. Once you connect with the potential hires, ask for references from them. Do your homework and contact, via telephone, those references they provide. Ask those references questions to help you decide if the potential hire is the right fit for your child and family. Remember, you will be leaving your precious children in the hired one's care.

Fully interview your daycare facility options, and make an appointment to visit with or without your child. Interview the director. Ask questions: how many children are assigned to each adult caregiver? How does the daycare center handle discipline? What is the facility's protocol if a child is sick? What does a typical day look like? What is the daycare facility's mission? How much time is spent indoors versus outside? What teaching or care credentials do the staff maintain? Observe the adults and their interaction with the children. How do the staff collaborate with one another and interact with the children in their care? Do you see happy or unhappy children?

With regard to in-home childcare, once hired, on paper write down for the sitter or nanny what your expectations are for the time they spend with your children. Share your family rules, schedules, food expectations, health issues, and how you expect them to interact with your children. Be specific. The hired caregiver may have their own ideas about what they will do while you are gone. If you have expectations or suggestions for them, write them out and discuss the activities. In addition, be flexible. The new caregiver may be a great cook, artist, basketball player, or dancer, and want to share those activities with your children. Consider those caregivers a diamond in the rough.

My children rarely watched television when they were little, so when we had a babysitter, I asked that they not watch TV, but rather play, dress up, color, craft, or go outside. When we returned from a well-deserved date night, I always asked the children what they had done while the babysitter had been with them. I most regret the one babysitter, who during her first visit to our home, put our one-year-old and nearly three-year-old in front of the television the entire three hours we were gone. Upon our return the three-year-old asked, "Mommy, what's 'annoying'?" The baby, who rarely cried and was always happy, screamed for two hours uncontrollably. To this day, I wonder if the sitter hurt the baby. Needless to say, something was not right. I had to go with my gut feeling, and the sitter was never asked back into our home.

Talk to your kids when you rejoin them at home. Be open to their honesty. Young children rarely lie. If you return home and something does not feel right, go with your gut feeling and find a new babysitter. No mental or physical damage to your children or physical damage to your home, no matter how insignificant, is worth a date night out. Find a different dependable babysitter, one you can trust with your children, for workdays or when you take a night off with your significant other.

You are the parent, caregiver, or teacher. Advocating for your children will require great amounts of time and effort, whether they are in school, enjoying extracurricular activities, or spending time with outside caregivers such as a babysitter. Remember, you get one chance to raise your children, so set good examples and support them to the best of your ability. Make nutrition and sleep a priority in your home. Educate yourself on topics affecting your children and their education, as well as the materials used.

To help you show up and to further assist you on the marvelous journey of being a parent, caregiver, or teacher, Lesson #6 offers valuable suggestions and resources to simplify schedules, gain knowledge, organize, teach, enjoy, and keep children safe.

Lesson #6

What's in Your Toolbox? Tips, Organization, Resources

The moment between what you once were and who you are becoming is where the dance of life really begins. — Barbara De Angelis

The extremely rewarding, yet demanding profession of parenting, teaching, and caregiving is an ongoing learning exercise. Like the children you guide, always strive to learn more. Make expanding your parent knowledge base a priority so that you find tools that will assist, simplify, and improve your parenting skills. Fill your parenting toolbox with concepts that work for your family, while discarding ideas that aren't the right fit. In this chapter you'll find a few tips for building your toolbox. The areas the tips address are playgroups, the local library, calendars, chores, safety, and family traditions.

Playgroups

Jon Berghoff, founder of XCHANGE, explained to Hal Elrod in episode 415 of Elrod's podcast that when a group of people is brought together, there is a measurable collective wisdom available from all parties: "The idea that one of us has all the answers is an outdated perspective on learning. Everyone has value in their thoughts, their perspectives, their experiences, their motivations." Playgroups act as one of these valuable information-gathering places that Berghoff was describing. Playgroups provide great exchanges of parenting information and experiences for the adults while also helping young children learn and practice their social skills.

When your children are young, socializing with children outside of your home environment is important. Children can learn and practice the same rules they learn in the home, but the dynamics are different. For young children, small playgroups with just a few children are best. Start your own playgroup either with friends and/or parents of children in your child's class. Playgroups are a great activity for preschoolers' socialization skills, as well as a wonderful way for parents to get to know other parents.

Once in elementary school, continue expanding your circle of parent and caregiver friends, colleagues, and support systems. One suggestion is to plan a group activity at the start of each school year such as a parents' coffee or family night. You could host the activity in your home or at the local library, community center, or coffee shop. These social events do not have to be fancy. The goal is for parents to meet other parents in their children's class.

Always remember that there will be people who cannot attend at certain times due to work commitments. Plan accordingly so that all parents can feel welcome. For example, in August, plan a morning coffee.

When you invite parents, acknowledge the fact that everyone's schedules vary, and point out if a parent cannot make it to a morning coffee, perhaps they can join the next month for an afternoon tea or an evening of appetizers.

Another option, plan a weekend picnic and invite all the families in your child's class to meet at a local park. During winter months, plan a family sledding or skating party complete with hot cocoa and marshmallows in the crisp, fresh air. Utilizing neighborhood public parks for gatherings requires little to no cost to organizers and parents. However, if you plan to use a park shelter, be sure to reserve the space ahead of time so that the shelter is available on your designated activity day.

Parents and caregivers can bring their own snacks or picnic supplies or sign up to bring a dish for a potluck meal. Be sure that each family is aware that they are responsible for the supervision, care, and safety of their own child. Providing childcare expectations within the invitation sets the stage that this is a family activity to be enjoyed together, not babysitting for parents who cannot attend.

Remember that the people you are inviting may be new to these activities and may forget to bring needed supplies for their families. It is always a good idea to provide a list of suggested items for caregivers to bring such as food, water, snacks, warm clothes, boots, mittens, hat, sled, skates, fishing poles, yard games (whatever the event entails), and remind them to dress accordingly for the weather.

You may be surprised at the results when you do not provide suggestions or a list. At a first grade day-long, outdoor education field trip held in January in a Midwest forest preserve, I was shocked to see that out of 26 first graders, only three or four children wore snow pants and winter boots. How does a child learn or enjoy a beautiful crisp winter day when they are not wearing proper clothing? The responsibility for children showing up prepared, clothing-wise, belongs to the teacher, the parents, and the child. Plan ahead!

Local Library

Another great free resource is your local library. Think back to your childhood. Go back to the basics and take a family field trip to this old-school venue. Visit your local library with children of all ages. Libraries are free and offer quiet and calming areas for everyone. Libraries are forgotten family gems due to technology today. Summer reading programs, toddler programs, adult programs, computer classes, etc., are all available at your local library. Most programs are free.

Librarians tend to be extremely helpful in finding every piece of literature on parenting, childcare, and education, as well as most other topics. If the library does not have what you are looking for, the librarian can help search and locate available materials online and from other libraries. With libraries at your fingertips, there is a significantly reduced need to order books from the internet, especially for children. Remember, as mentioned already, I urge you to stay within your family's budget.

Take the kids, get out of the house, and search for free books or materials through your local library. Children love the library. Visit the children's department where they will thoroughly enjoy perusing the multitude of books in the children's sections. Also explore other areas in the library so that your children see the vast array of learning and enjoyment materials available to them as they grow and mature.

Checking out books from the library fosters responsibility and accountability in children and brings the family back to explore and experience more literature at another time. Enjoying and taking care of books that belong to the library helps children learn to care for materials, as well as supports the importance of reading. Weekly library visits build a love for libraries and reading that lasts into adulthood.

To help cultivate that love of reading and the importance of taking care of belongings such as library books, together decorate a cloth bag with your child's name. Then each time your family plans a visit to the library, use the child's own special book bag to transport books back and forth. This simple exercise is a precursor for your young child to the future time when they will begin transporting school materials back and forth in their backpacks. Keep library books and your child's specific book bag in a spot where your child can easily access the contents and you can remember to grab the library book bag on your return trip to the library.

Side note: visiting a library while out of town or on a trip is another free and fun experience when you have extra time and are looking for simple child-appropriate activities. You will not be able to check out books to take with you, but you can still experience all the library has to offer within its walls. This same free option is available to your family if you live outside of a library district and your taxes do not support the nearest library. You and your family can utilize the free library materials, but you will not be allowed to take those materials home.

Other available free resources include your local parks and recreational areas. Fresh air experienced in nature adds health into every day. Whether you live in a large city, tiny town, or out in the country, get outside and check out what activities are available in your area. Fresh air is imperative to a healthy life, good sleep, and a calm soul. Consider daily walks, and visits to playgrounds, walking trails, park districts, conservation districts, historical societies, and YMCAs. Many of these offer affordable programs for children, and sometimes the curriculums are even free.

Contact these local organizations, check out their monthly calendar of events, and review their many offerings. These year-round activities are just one more opportunity and location for your child to meet other children and for you to connect with parents who have similar interests.

Calendars, Planning, and Packing

Calendars are a great idea for the whole family. Purchase or create a large calendar, and post it for the entire family to see. Have your children help create and decorate the calendar, as well as add their activities. Label all daily, weekly, and recurring activities; label all sports activities, lunch days, daycare days, preschool days, etc. Teach your child how to use the calendar. When your child knows the day's activities because they visually observe them on the calendar, daily planning and organization improve and potential anxiety is reduced. Don't agree to do an activity that you know you will not or cannot attend. It is far better to say ahead of time, "No, I am sorry, but we cannot attend that party on that day" or "We won't be able to make ballet that day."

Remember, accountability and reliability are very important at any age and especially in children. Do not lead on a child or get their hopes up by agreeing to do an activity that they want to do, knowing you are unable or unwilling to attend, and hoping the child will forget. Children will not forget, and it is highly likely that their interaction with other children will bring up the activity, furthering the reminder that children do not forget special activities on the calendar. If you sign up your child for an activity or RSVP to a party, be accountable. Show up on time. Plan ahead. Do not arrive late. Tardy arrivals are not okay, even if the event is a toddler's birthday party or tee ball game. Be considerate and punctual. Follow through with your word. Remember, your child is observing all of your behavior and from that observation, the youngster is learning how to behave in the world. Get your child to baseball on time. Whatever the activity, be accountable and dependable.

Equally important, always, always every day check your child's backpack for notes sent home, as well as the email account that you provided your child's teacher. Immediately add any school activities to the family calendar, using a marker color associated with that specific child. This simple color coordination on the calendar helps even small children check to see what activities they have that specific day and week. The color-coding system helps them read their own schedule and allows you to quickly evaluate and plan your day.

For each child, create a "To/From School" folder with pockets to keep in their backpack. Write on the front cover of the folder "School Notes." Inside, on the left pocket of the folder, write "To school." On the right-side folder pocket, write "From school." When you have notes to send to the teacher, put them in the "To school" side of the folder. Practice with your young child, act out, or pretend what to do with the folder and note when they arrive at school, so they know what to do. This practice may seem so simple and an obvious action to do with a note, but many children simply do not understand the value of turning in materials. Thus, make a game out of turning in a note or homework. Act it out. Make it fun. Then practice what the child should do when they receive notes or work to be sent home.

At the end of the school day, your child should put notes or homework pages in the "From school" side of the folder to be unpacked when home and in your company. As a parent, check the "To/From" folder every day right when your child returns home. Start this important habit early so that children learn and recognize that school and homework are important and that the materials traveling back and forth disseminate important information to your family. If you receive notes or permission slips that require a response or payment, fill them out immediately or while your child is having their after-school snack. Make note of the field trip date or class presentation on the family calendar. Next, insert return forms and payments in the "To school" folder pocket and then remind your child to turn it in during the next class period. With smaller children, this reminder should be repeated when dropping the child off at school.

Do not wait until bedtime to open the backpack and take care of school business. Both child and parent are tired by this time. Failing to check the backpack immediately and on a daily basis is a scheduling disaster waiting to happen. You would feel terrible if you missed your daughter's Daisy Troop Halloween hayride at the pumpkin farm or your three-year-old's preschool apple picking field trip at the orchard. Back to basics: it's simple; check the backpack every day, as well as the emails from school when your child arrives home from school. Then take care of school business.

Whether you are a paper scheduler or a tech savvy organizer, plan and organize a binder (physical or on your computer) for each school year. The binder should have section dividers so that you can organize your child's school year. Different sections might include medical forms, school calendar, important notes (like permission slips), class lists and phone numbers, room parent responsibilities, class photos, special school projects (that your child creates), clubs and activities. As your child grows, this single binder concept may evolve, depending on what and how many activities in which your child participates.

Depending on your child's school, your child may bring home enormous amounts of art projects and paperwork or very little. If there are certain "creations" you would like to keep but do not have the space to store or display around the home, take a photo and file the photo in your child's yearly school folder. (This is what the above-mentioned "special school projects" section is for.) If you want to enjoy the creation for a period of time, hang it on the wall or refrigerator, and when a new project arrives, have the child help you take down the old creation for filing. Have the child file the old creation or the photo of their work in the school binder if they so choose. If the child chooses to discard the old work, allow them to do so. Periodically, peruse through your child's school binder and discard old permission slips and newsletters to keep the binder manageable. At the end of each school year, the child will have fun going through that year's binder and discarding unwanted pictures, papers, etc. Repeat the yearly binder process each year to keep the school information organized.

Another tip: children are never too young to learn to help pack their snacks, lunches, and backpacks for the following school day. Make an assembly line of what goes into the lunch bag or snack sack. The idea here is to begin teaching children how to help themselves and give them some responsibility and potentially some self-pride in accomplishing tasks for the following school day. With supervision, practicing these self-sufficiency skills over time will assist your child in their independence and growth from childhood to adulthood.

Routines: Morning and Bedtime

To help develop organizational habits such as before bedtime routines or morning routines, depending on your child's age, create a morning/nighttime board. This is a simple hands-on visual that children can be involved in creating. For example, an eight-by-ten-inch (or any size) magnetic dry-erase board works well. Split the board into four even quadrants. Working clockwise and using a permanent marker, draw a sun in the first quadrant to indicate morning actions. In the second quadrant to the right draw a check mark. This area will be used when the morning actions are complete. In the quadrant beneath the morning sun, draw a moon for nighttime actions. In the fourth quadrant to the right of the moon quadrant, draw a check mark; when filled, this fourth quadrant will signify that the nighttime actions have been completed. Display the board in your child's room where it is easily accessible to your child.

Create small pictures or symbols of the tasks to be completed. You can use small round magnets to attach these pictures to the board. For example, for morning tasks include a picture of a coat hook (reminder to hang up jammies in the closet), clothes (get dressed), toothbrush and washcloth (brush teeth, wash face), and bed (make your bed). The evening/moon task magnets might include a picture of a toothbrush and washcloth, a toilet, PJs, clothes (reminder to set out clothes for the next day). Each nighttime symbol should identify the important tasks to be completed each evening.

Demonstrate and practice using the magnets with your child. To start, all symbol magnets should be in the morning sun quadrant or evening moon quadrant. As your child completes each task, have them move the magnets from the sun or moon side to the completed check mark side. As the parent or caregiver, your job will be to replace the magnets to the sun or moon side so that the chart is ready for the next morning or bedtime routine.

In our home, we called this board the blessing board. We blessed ourselves by taking care of ourselves at bedtime and in the morning. We also blessed our rooms by making our beds each day so that when we returned to our bed at night, it blessed us back by creating a visually organized, pleasing, and welcoming space for us to crawl into and sleep.

Helping Around the House

Similar to the blessing board, the chore board (or whatever name you choose) acts as a reminder of important tasks that need to be completed. As children grow older and you want to teach the contract concept rather than allowances (from Lesson #2), the chore board is a good place to start. These jobs could be the tasks you want your child to conduct on Saturday mornings or another day during the week. Again, the chores should be age-specific and the child should be able to complete the task, preferably without help. After all, this activity is supposed to help children grow to be more independent. By checking off each task on a laminated list or moving a magnet from the "chores to do" side to the "chores are finished/check mark" side, you provide a visual reminder of tasks to be done or that have been completed, which creates foundational organizing skills and can instill in your child the simple satisfaction, usually subconsciously, that they have completed and accomplished some order of business that day.

Make a game out of washing non-breakable dishes and non-sharp utensils. This inexpensive, child-calming activity involves bubbles, water, and perhaps a large bath towel on the floor. The bonus is clean dishes, and the child learns a simple skill they will use their entire lives. Practice with them. Demonstrate scrubbing the bowls, wiping up the spills, drying the kitchen items, and setting them aside to finish air drying. Give children a sponge and a spray bottle of water. Show them how you clean off the counter or vanity.

Play upbeat music, provide children with a colorful duster or dust cloth, and make chore-type activities, such as dusting and cleaning, fun. Have the children help sort laundry into dark and light colors, or put all the blue clothes in one pile, the red in another, and the white in another, etc. How many kids head off to college and throw all colors together into the washing machine, ruining an entire load of laundry? This simple sorting process, started as a game in childhood, might sometime in the future save your college student the embarrassment of pink boxer shorts because he learned to sort colors as a toddler ... just saying.

Demonstrating and teaching children how and where to put clothes away into drawers or a closet, as well as putting toys away where they belong, are skills all parents and teachers want children to learn. Remember, children are always learning, so be patient and understand that perfection is not the goal, rather learning and being able to apply the concept independently are most important. The "clean-up-or-put-away" process can be made easier for children by using laminated pictures (combined with words) on labels that are attached to toy bins, closet shelves, etc. Just like matching games, the labeled boxes, bins, or shelves provide children with a visual cue for where to put items away. Toys you want sorted have the laminated photo of what item goes in each bin, making the job easier for you and your children. Sorting items such as clothes, or toys, or putting away non-sharp silverware helps children notice differences and likenesses and helps with one-to-one correlations. Believe it or not, these types of activities help develop your child's large and small motor skills, spatial awareness, as well as concentration, focus, and brain function.

Learning organization and self-sufficiency through simple family chores can start at any age. Remember, children are always watching and learning from your behaviors. Teaching young children how to care for themselves, their belongings, their surroundings, and other people are skills that will blossom as they grow into adolescents and young adults. Simple age-appropriate chores can be very fulfilling and rewarding for children and set them up for future learning and self-care.

No Getting Lost

Never make rash decisions based on fear. Instead, make decisions based on fact. "There is no need to be afraid of the monster under the bed if the mattress is on the floor," someone once said. Do not scare, rather prepare.

Parents can prepare their children ahead of time and remind them before vacations or trips to the mall, etc., the importance of staying safe by remaining close to the adult in charge. Discuss with your children what they should do if they get separated and believe that they are lost. For example, if you are headed to the mall, tell your children if they get separated, to ask for help from a mother with children, a security guard, or a woman working at the counter. On vacation, for example, if separated on the ski hill, the child should ask for help from a ski patrol, chairlift operator, or a mother with children. Again, preparing children the best you can ahead of time gives them options for helping themselves if needed.

Never turn your back on a child or leave a child in a grocery cart in public. All it takes is a second for a child to wander or—heaven forbid—be abducted. Equally important is to never make light of the situation if your toddler does walk away. Never play the "cat and mouse game" when a toddler hides from you behind a clothes rack, for example. This dangerous behavior must be stopped and redirected immediately so that the child never forms a habit of walking away or hiding from you.

Chasing the child provides them with attention in a negative manner, in a potentially dangerous setting.

Instead, always use proactive, positive reinforcement with verbal cues when out in public with all children. Say to children, "I really like that you are being safe today at the store by staying close to me." Periodically reminding them of this behavior helps prevent the opposite from occurring. Remember, children love praise. Redirecting potential runaway behavior when you sense the behavior is about to occur to a positive behavior is another method for keeping the child safe and close to the adult in charge.

When our children were learning to walk in toddler shoes, they were delighted by and enjoyed little metal bells woven onto their shoelaces (once the children were past the "putting-small-objects-in-their-mouths" phase, of course). These bells also were helpful when shopping and while out in public since they gave off a quiet jingle with the pitter patter of little feet. And thus, we could always hear where our children were located.

Fire Safety

Once your children begin attending preschool and elementary school, they will practice different safety situations including fire drills, tornado drills, etc. Fire safety month is October and a great month to annually change smoke detector batteries. In school, children will practice fire drills and will likely visit the local fire station for a field trip. Take this learning opportunity to also practice your own fire drill at home. Set a "fire meeting spot" outside of the home and explain why that is a good location if there ever is a fire in the house. Choose a "fire meeting spot" location that is far enough away from the house, but within sight for firemen, etc., for example, the mailbox at the end of the driveway. Talk to your children about feeling the back of doors with the back of their hands and crawling to avoid smoke. Discuss how to get to that fire meeting spot from different rooms in the house. Teaching children about fire safety should not scare them, but rather prepare them in case the situation arises.

Safety at a Friend's House

As children age, they will spend more time away from home playing with other children. Before allowing your children to play elsewhere be sure that you are comfortable with the family with whom your child will be playing. Do not assume all households are alike. There is a fine line when it comes to being overprotective versus simply making sure your child will be safe at a playdate outside of your home. At first and when children are young, stay for a bit or the entire time with your child. Observe how the children interact. You should always offer that option to parents when their children come to play at your home as well. This is an easy way to determine whether the children are a good fit for one another and if the other family is like-minded when it comes to safe child's play and parenting.

When your children are old enough, it is a good idea to discuss what to do if they are not feeling comfortable or safe when they are spending time with a friend away from their own home. A very wise mother and friend had a code word/sentence that she and her child agreed upon. If her child did not feel safe or wanted to get out of an uncomfortable situation (perhaps the other children were getting into trouble and her son wanted out), the son would ask to use a phone, call home, and give the mom the code word/phrase or question. The code phrase her family used was, "Are we having cake tonight?" When the mother heard that question, she knew her son needed help or an early pickup. The phrase could be asked over the phone without anyone near her son knowing what was going on; he could ask for adult help without having to say so out loud. Again, do not scare your children, rather prepare them, and give them tools they can use to help themselves in difficult situations.

Love Languages and Endearing Family Traditions

In Audrey Penn's book *The Kissing Hand*, Chester raccoon's mother reminds him that her kisses are in his hand as that is where she placed one when she told Chester the secret that her mother told her long, long ago. Chester's mother explains that whenever he feels lonely and thinks he needs a little loving from home, "Just press your hand to your cheek and think, 'Mommy loves you,' and that kiss will stay with you wherever you go, no matter how many times you wash your hands." Chester, too, gave his mom a kiss on her fan-spread hand so that she would always have his kiss as well.

This often-read, lovely children's book is a great way to start your child's school year and a nice family tradition to repeat yearly. Read the book at home and practice the technique to reassure young children that you are always thinking of them. You will be amazed how long your children remember the special "kissing hand" routine, especially if implemented and used often.

Create and employ other love languages specific to your own family for when children need extra support or love. Offer a hug-a-thon or family group hug, create your own method, and call it what you will, for when a child has had a tough day. Make sure you use and reuse the family's chosen method in times of need so that your child learns to relax and perhaps feels, as a result of your family's special hug, your expression of love.

The following is a great example from an unknown author. The story goes like this: "I had a child who was just coming unraveled in every way today. He walked up to me and said, 'Today just isn't so good.' I sighed, looked him in the eye, and said, "Can I give you a one-minute hug?' He shrugged and said, 'I guess.' I said, 'You have to commit for the whole minute, can you do that?' He said, 'I guess.' So, the hug began. At 20 seconds (I always watch the clock), he whispered, 'Why one minute?' I whispered back, 'So my heart can talk to yours.' By 30 seconds his squeeze tightened and by 45 seconds his head was on my shoulder. At 60 seconds I said, 'You made it.' He didn't move. Ten more seconds passed. I said, 'It's time.' He said, 'Thanks for talking to my heart,' looked me in the eye, and half-smiled. Who knows what tomorrow will bring, but today that child was loved if only for 70 seconds. Love them all. Period.' Create your own loving gesture to provide extra love for your children during stressful times.

Saving Memorabilia—I touched on this briefly in this chapter and now let's visit it with a deeper look. As hard as it may seem, tell yourself that you do not need to record and keep every craft, school paper, or award that your child receives. Be proactive and choose to select the best to keep and discard the rest. Involve your children in the selection process. You may be surprised to learn that the one item you think is the best is not the picture or craft that your child wants to keep. Conduct this "sort-keep-or-discard" activity often, perhaps weekly or monthly. Do not put off the task.

Depending on how much material your child brings home from preschool and elementary school, you may acquire piles of projects. Taking photos of special projects and creating a book of those projects is another space-saving option. Saving too much material memorabilia from year to year simply creates an overwhelming purging process later in life. And at that time, your child may or may not even remember the project or its purpose.

For an easy and space-saving way to save memories, write down the funny sayings your toddlers or kids verbalize or display. You will love looking back years later remembering and reading those precious words. Do not worry about perfection. Make time to write in a journal, as well as complete a baby book for each child. Again, baby books do not need to be perfect or fancy; however, be sure to complete one for each child or create one family book with each child's information.

In today's high-tech world, complete with cloud storage, experts say that there will be entire generations whose family history will be lost because no one made a hard copy of family photos or kept paper records of births, deaths, marriages, medical histories, etc. Do not put off creating a simple hard copy record of your child's birth because perfection is holding you back. Simply get it done, and then enjoy watching your child grow, adding pertinent information along the way into the "old-fashioned" baby book.

If you are not attentive to this concept, you will find that the first child gets everything saved and written down, and the second child hardly has anything. Both kids turn out the way God wants them to turn out and having the perfect baby book is not a sign of how well or poorly your child will succeed. Consider, for example, by age two, our first child had 19 photo albums. After seven years of brutal infertility treatment and disappointments, I wanted to document every movement, activity, and cute face my first child possessed. When child number one was two years, nine months old, we were blessed with our second child. How would I keep up with the photo journaling of child number two and number one at the same time?

I might add that my children were born before cell phones contained cameras. This meant I had to have actual film in a camera (later, on an SD card), then I had to drive to the camera shop (do these even exist anymore?). At the store, I had to turn in the film (later, upload my SD card) for processing. Photo processing took several days, so it could take a week for the store to print the photos. Again, this was before digital photos were invented, so you did not know what your photos looked like before printing, and you had to print and pay for all of them. The following week involved putting two kids in car seats, driving to the camera shop, and picking up the photos. Next, I sorted the photos and put them into photo albums. Never did I throw out the bad photos. No, I just put them all into photo albums with the plastic pages. Why? Because I was trying to capture everything having to do with my two darling children.

Tell me this, what will my now older and grownup, still-darling child do with those 19 photo albums covering ages zero to age two? Don't forget there were albums that followed those 19 as well. And, of course, child number two had photo albums, just not as many. The point of this story is for you to think about what memories you are preserving and how you are preserving them. Consider what you save for them and for yourself, as well as the amount, so that memorabilia is a gift and not a burden—an overwhelming project someone later must go through, sort, and decide to save or discard.

Sometimes it makes a parent sad to think that their children will someday grow up and move out of the house. But that is reality. Don't waste your time, energy, or mindset being sad. This negative approach is unhealthy, causes stress, inhibits proper positive parenting, and, thus, isn't in the best interest of your child. Instead, live your parenting life to its fullest. Remember, each day with your children is a gift. Be present always when you are with your children. Handle distractions that keep you from being your best parenting self. Parenting is an unparalleled opportunity. Your job as a parent, caregiver, or teacher is to prepare, teach, and lead your children as they grow to be independent, self-sufficient young adults. The opposite would be doing your children a disservice. How would your children survive? Proper parenting prepares children so that they can lead life on their own someday. If you give parenting and your children your best self every single day, you will never look back on life with regret. So, put a smile on your face and in your heart as you embrace the parenting challenge, knowing you are making a difference in your child's life every single day.

With your toolbox full of these organizational tips, strategies, and resources, as well as others you find along the way, you will be better prepared as a parent, teacher, or caregiver. Equally important is to make time to care for yourself, so that you start each day refreshed and renewed. In the next chapter, we will look at what inspires you to keep going when times are tough, recommendations for maintaining a healthy mindset, and suggestions to help perpetuate your grit and greatness.

Lesson #7

Where Do You Get Your Inspiration? Build Yourself Up

An extraordinary life is all about daily, continuous improvements in the areas that matter most. — Robin Sharma

Where do you get your strength? How do you build your confidence? What gets you going and keeps you going every day? Everyone, and every family, has issues and difficulties at times. That is the story of life. We have ups, we have downs. How do you best handle situations and carry on? Build and maintain your positive mindset, and be open to continual learning, self-support, and perseverance. Without challenges, life would be boring, and no one would ever learn new strategies and ideas. Everyone needs support when faced with challenges.

As parents, caregivers, and educators, it is vitally important to realize that you are not alone and that other people and families have experienced many of the same hardships that you and your family or classroom may be experiencing right now. Take a deep breath, acknowledge issues, create solutions, and keep your mindset light while remembering you are among others experiencing the same situations. Like the Zac Brown Band song says, "We are all in the same boat." Remind yourself that you are capable and that you are not alone. There are resources available to assist you with whatever your family or classroom is currently experiencing.

Read on for ideas on finding your own personal inspiration. Utilizing podcasts, setting goals, and scheduling time for yourself are just a few suggestions for sourcing that inspiration. Find what influences guide you best to "handle and carry on" in the face of adversity and challenge. Then use those methods to develop and maintain the best version of yourself so that you can be the best parent, teacher, or caregiver possible.

The Source of Your Inspiration

When life gets challenging, keep a positive mindset. Maintain an open mind and allow yourself time to search for what inspires you to learn more. What helps you learn and get things done when you don't feel like it? Where do you get your inspiration? Is it from a song or in a quote? Is it from the instructor at your workout class? Is it the mantra on the wall at the yoga studio? Is it simply working out? Is it your best friend who always stays positive and seems to have an answer for everything? Is it kind words from your parish priest, reverend, or rabbi? Is it your favorite inspirational book?

A Cascade of Podcasts

The podcast industry has a wealth of health and happiness offerings from the scientific to the whimsical, including new names, as well as tried and

true life stories from older and wiser mentors. On a recent *Living &
Learning with Reba McEntire* podcast, Ms. McEntire interviewed the
bubbly and world-famous country singer, actress, and businesswoman
Dolly Parton, who grew up financially poor but spiritually blessed
with positivity. The iconic Ms. Parton shared her five life lessons for
individuals at any age:

1. To thine own self be true. In today's society, there are lots
   of people and concepts coming at you from all around. Stay
   focused on who you are at the core. You know you and what
   is right. Be yourself. Don't be a fake.

2. Never ignore your roots, your home, or your hair.

3. A loose tongue can lead to broken teeth.

4. Prayer is not a formal affair … It's more come as you are.

5. Anyone who says you can't take it with you hasn't seen me pack.

Find what support and inspiration systems work best for you and
embrace those networks that inspire you as a parent and as an individual.
Find the humor and lightness in issues that arise, and allow grace to guide
you to solutions.

Goal Setting and Scheduling

Organizing your life and mindset are worthwhile, effective, and calming.
Set yearly, monthly, and daily goals for yourself. Write down those goals,
and revisit and finetune them often. Hal Elrod, in episode 407 of his

podcast, suggests setting goals in these areas of your life: health (and mental health) and fitness, finance, career or business, relationships, contributions and giving, personal development, and fun and relaxation. Make time for fun and relaxation each day to help build your sense of self. Planning goals, including rest and relaxation into each day, and scheduling the activities on your daily calendar allows you to budget your time for everything on your to-do list for that day.

When you schedule yourself a daily break from work, family commitments, etc., because you have "calendar-scheduled" that break activity into the day, you end up returning to your day-to-day responsibilities with a renewed mind and spirit. Taking well-needed breaks is important for all parties involved. Until the end of time there will be work to do, laundry to wash, grass to cut, meals to make, garages to clean, kid activities to attend. By taking time for yourself daily, you can be present for those other equally important responsibilities.

In addition to making time for yourself, regularly plan into your schedule some "alone time" or a "date night" for you and your significant other. Life well-lived requires balance. Life is never perfect. All each of us can do is keep showing up. Taking a break to refresh and revitalize relationships makes parenting and caregiving that much easier because you have taken time to care for yourself and your significant other, the person who helped you bring your children into this world.

Since life is not perfect, mistakes happen. Never beat yourself up when you make mistakes. In David Goggins' inspiring memoir, *Can't Hurt Me*, he reminds his audience that people make mistakes and poor choices, and in fact all people at some time in life make mistakes and poor choices. The author explains through his life experiences that people should never make excuses for mistakes or feel sorry for themselves for the life situations they are handed. Goggins' childhood was filled with disappointment, poverty, prejudice, and physical abuse. Through his hard work, dedication, self-discipline, and mental toughness he overcame his overweight, depressed self, as well as his "going nowhere" victim mentality. Resilience is defined as the capacity of a person to maintain their core purpose and integrity in the face of dramatically changed circumstances. Goggins taught himself resilience and transformed himself into a US Armed Forces icon, a world-famous top athlete, and an author.

"The 40 Percent Rule" in Goggins' book outlines the fact that most people give up when they have only given 40 percent of their effort towards a goal. This statistic reminds us that we all have another 60 percent available to utilize. Do not get comfortable, stick with the process, persist, and pursue greatness! Never take on pitying yourself or employing a victim mentality. Instead, acknowledge the error or issue, learn from the situation, work hard to overcome the mistake, move on, and most importantly persevere to remain mentally tough. As Goggins says, "The bottom line is that life is one big mind game. The only person you are playing against is yourself." Stand firm and press on. Don't stop at 40 percent. Apply that next 60 percent. Give life, parenting, and teaching 100 percent every single day.

It's Already There

You have inside of you everything you need to get through any difficult situation. Own that statement and commit the thought to your memory. The famous author Norman Vincent Peale conducted studies acknowledging that a person is capable of accomplishing any goal or overcoming any challenge as long as that person wrote it down and repeated the goal or affirmation over and over. The statement was then committed to the person's deep memory. One example that Peale used personally and mentioned in his book, *The Power of Positive Thinking*, was that when faced with fear, anxiety, or insecurity, he would say to himself his own previously-memorized statement, "I can do all things through Christ who strengthens me." Try utilizing the strategy. Create your own affirmations or copy Mr. Peale's bible verse from Philippians 4:13 when addressing challenges, whether those situations affect you individually or your family as a whole.

Make sure to look for the good in each of those challenging circumstances. Surround yourself with people who make you a better version of yourself through their support and positive encouragement. Search for, find, and employ resources, books, podcasts, quotes, etc., that resonate with you and help you maintain your positive mindset and continual learning.

In Admiral William H. McRaven's book *Hero Code*, he states:

> I came to realize that there is a hero in all of us. There is an innate code that has been there since the birth of mankind. It is written in our DNA. It is what drove the great expansion of humanity out of Africa. It summoned the explorers to cross the deserts and the seas. It helped create the great faiths. It emboldened the early scientists and philosophers. It nurtured the ill and infirm. It spoke truth to the masses. It brought order to chaos and hope to the desperate. This code is not a cipher, or a cryptograph, or a puzzle to be solved. It is a moral code, an internal code of conduct that drives the human race to explore, to nurture, to comfort, to inspire, and to laugh so that societies can flourish.

You have innately within you that hero code. Embrace the hero code and utilize that inherent knowledge to further build and continuously strengthen your own personal development, as well as foster positivity in people around you.

Focus, nurture, and optimize your social, emotional, mental, physical, and spiritual capabilities through continuous self-education and personal development in the areas you enjoy, as well as areas that challenge you. Take what you like and use it to improve your parenting, caregiving, and teaching. Discard ideas that do not work for you, your family, or your particular situation.

The following are just a few resource suggestions and types for further exploration as a parent, caregiver, or teacher on the topics discussed:

- *All I Really Need to Know I Learned in Kindergarten* by Robert Fulghum

- *Can't Hurt Me—Master Your Mind and Defy the Odds* by David Goggins

- "Country Again," a song by Thomas Rhett

- Dave Ramsey Solutions, commonsense finance tips: daveramseysolutions.com

- *The Five Choices—The Path to Extraordinary Productivity* by Franklin Covey

- *The Hero Code* by Admiral William H. McRaven

- *Make Your Bed* by Admiral William H. McRaven

- *The Miracle Morning/The Miracle Equation* by Hal Elrod

- Optimize/heroic.com

- *The Power of Positive Thinking* by Norman Vincent Peale

- *Starting Your Day Right* by Joyce Meyer

- *Who Do We Choose to Be—Facing Reality, Claiming Leadership, Restoring Sanity* by Margaret J. Wheatley

Knowledge is power. No matter your age, socioeconomic status, or background, you can always learn more whether that learning relates to self-improvement, parenting, teaching, organizing, fitness, finances—whatever the topic. No one but you can stop you from improving yourself through continuous learning. Make learning a priority. Invest in yourself. Instead of wasting precious time binge-watching television or falling into the deep, dark hole of social media, empower yourself with learning more. Find your inspiration. Say to yourself, "Tonight, instead of watching that addictive series, I am going to do something to better myself because I am worth it! I am going to go for a walk [or listen to a positive podcast, read that book I've always wanted to read, review my goals, write three things I am grateful for in my gratitude journal]." Use your brain and your senses to better yourself. Find resources that resonate with you and inspire you. Your time and your life will be more rewarding and are more valuable when you spend time empowering yourself with knowledge.

Taking care of yourself, as well as finding and utilizing resources that inspire you, will help you be a better parent, teacher, and caregiver. Keep an ongoing list (perhaps on your phone) of the resources, books, podcasts, songs, quotes, slogans, and such that inspire you. Include recommendations you hear about that you think might help you build yourself up, teach you more about parenting or caregiving, as well as resources that have helped you to date. When you are with others and they seem to be searching for answers, items on your list may help them. Share the knowledge and be open to learning more from others' recommendations through these valuable information exchanges. On that note, my next chapter reminds us of the importance and value of collective wisdom, the cooperative mindset, and the ever-important topic woven throughout this book—continual learning.

Conclusion

Collective Wisdom, Cooperative Mindset, and Continuous Learning

Alone we can do so little, together we can do so much. — Helen Keller

The concept of collective wisdom motivated me to write this book. What I mean by that is that no one person has all the answers to any situation when dealing with parenting, teaching, or raising children. When people gather to share their history, experiences, and knowledge for the betterment of society or to solve one tiny problem, everyone benefits. Individuals can take that sifted knowledge and utilize its best points for their own personal development and growth.

Cooperative mindset and learning from a variety of sources provide the answer for parental and personal development. Embrace and winnow the wealth of information and resources that are available to you. You are the master of your own domain, and you are capable of being the best parent, caregiver, or teacher that you can be. Go forth and seek out knowledge from all sources. Learn from your mistakes, and with grace improve your parenting, caregiving, and teaching. There is no such thing as a perfect parent, caregiver, or teacher. However, the best parents, teachers, and caregivers are open to continuous learning, improving, and showing up with grace and grit every single day.

We are lucky to live in this country full of freedoms, the great United States of America. Here, you and I have freedoms that families just like ours but in other countries only dream about. Here we have the freedom to choose, the freedom to work, the freedom to learn, the freedom to educate, and many other freedoms too numerous to mention. We have the right to learn more to become a better parent and teacher.

Know your rights and use those rights to build yourself up, your children up, your students up, and all people around you up. Value those rights and protect them by staying current with what is occurring in your town, school, and country. Never allow anyone to take those rights away from you, your family, your children, or your students. Empower yourself with knowledge and experience so that you can build yourself up, and, thus, you can build up others around you and in your care. Be strong in your convictions to choose right over wrong and to advocate for your children. Pay close attention to schools and what they are teaching. Volunteer and support teachers in those learning environments with the beliefs you want your children to carry on to future generations. To thine own self be true!

In the book *The Road to Character* by David Brooks we read the following: "The resumé virtues are the ones you list on your resumé, the skills that ... contribute to external success. The eulogy virtues ... get talked about at your funeral ... whether you are kind, brave, honest, or faithful." Through your behaviors, you essentially write your own eulogy.

Life is about you making choices and sacrifices for the betterment of yourself and others in your circle of influence. The choice is yours. What do you want people to say about you at the end of your life? Would you prefer that your resumé virtues are the focus at your funeral or that your character and eulogy virtues are discussed at your celebration of life ceremony? What will your children eulogize about you?

Without being too philosophical, make parenting your priority, starting when your children are young and continuing until they leave the nest. You never get the time back as a parent, so do your best and handle the ups and downs with grace. If you always choose doing the right thing over the easy thing as a parent, caregiver, or teacher, you will look back on life with no regrets.

So, get to work. Be present, just breathe, build up your own personal parenting confidence and your child's confidence, show up for your children, get organized, utilize resources, seek out inspiration, share that wisdom with others, and live life full of grace.

Carpe diem! Seize the day! Go forth and be amazing!

References

An, H.-Y., Chen, W., Wang, C.-W., Yang, H.-F., Huang, W.-T., & Fan, S.-Y. (2020). The Relationships between Physical Activity and Life Satisfaction and Happiness among Young, Middle-Aged, and Older Adults. *International Journal of Environmental Research and Public Health, 17*(13), 4817.

Association of Waldorf Schools of North America. (n.d.). (2022). *Waldorf Education.*

Berghoff, J. (2022, January 7). *About.* XCHANGE.

Brooks, D. (2016). *The Road to Character.* Random House.

Covey, S. R. (2020). *The 7 Habits of Highly Effective People: 30th Anniversary Edition.* Simon & Schuster.

Duckworth, A. (2019). *Grit: The Power of Passion and Perseverance.* Vermilion.

Easterlin, R. A. (2003, September 4). Explaining happiness. *Proceedings of the National Academy of Sciences, 100*(19), 11176–11183.

Elrod, H. (Host). (2020, February 2). How To Lead Your Community with Jon Berghoff (No. 415) [Audio podcast episode]. In *Achieve Your Goals with Hal Elrod*.

Elrod, H. (Host). (2021, December 8). My Best Advice to Make 2022 Your Best Year Yet! (No. 407) [Audio podcast episode]. In *Achieve Your Goals with Hal Elrod*.

Goggins, D. (2018). *Can't Hurt Me: Master Your Mind and Defy the Odds*. Lioncrest Publishing.

Hales, D. (2019). *An Invitation to Health: Your Life, Your Future*. Cengage Learning.

Holtz, L. (2009). *Winning Every Day: The Game Plan for Success*. HarperCollins.

Kardaras, N. (2017). *Glow Kids: How Screen Addiction Is Hijacking Our Kids - and How to Break the Trance*. St. Martin's Griffin.

Kelly, M. (2015). *The Rhythm of Life: Living Every Day with Passion & Purpose*. Blue Sparrow Books.

Kenison, K. (2002). *Mitten Strings for God: Reflections for Mothers in a Hurry*. Grand Central Publishing.

Kenison, K. (2010). *The Gift of an Ordinary Day: A Mother's Memoir*. Grand Central Publishing.

Lembke, A. (2021). *Dopamine Nation: Finding Balance in the Age of Indulgence*. E. P. Dutton & Company, Inc.

Marcos, L. R. (2022, March 29). A Silent Tragedy. Retrieved from

McEntire, R. (Host). (2020, September 20). Forging Your Own Path with Dolly Parton (No. 2) [Audio podcast episode]. In *Living & Learning with Reba McEntire*.

McRaven, W. H. (2021). *The Hero Code: Lessons Learned from Lives Well Lived*. Grand Central Publishing, Hachette Book Group.

Miller, A., & Miller, B. (2019). *Play to Their Strengths: A New Approach to Parenting Your Kids as God Made Them*. Harvest House Publishers.

National Center for Education Statistics. (n.d.). *Bullying: How many students are bullied at school?* Retrieved 2019, from

National Center for Montessori in the Public Sector. (2022, May 20). *A National Hub for Public Montessori*.

Orlowski-Yang, J. (Director). (2020). *The Social Dilemma* [Film]. Exposure Labs; Argent Pictures; The Space Program.

Peale, N. V. (2011). *The Power of Positive Thinking*. Ishi Press.

Penn, A. (1993). *The Kissing Hand*. Child Welfare League of America.

University of Notre Dame. (2022, April 28). *A Conversation with Condoleezza Rice* [Video]. YouTube. .

Weisberg, D. S., Hirsh-Pasek, K., Golinkoff, R. M., Kittredge, A. K., & Klahr, D. (2016). Guided Play: Principles and Practices. *Current Directions in Psychological Science, 25*(3), 177–182.

Wheatley, M. J. (2017). *Who Do We Choose to Be? Facing Reality, Claiming Leadership, Restoring Sanity*. Berrett-Koehler Publishers, Inc.
Wyma, K. W. (2015). *I'm Happy for You (Sort Of...Not Really): Finding Contentment in a Culture of Comparison*. WaterBrook Press.

Acknowledgments

Thank you to the people who made a difference in my life without knowing it ...

My mom—who sacrificed fashion at times by wearing our old sweaters, for penny pinching for our family, for setting an example by volunteering at school and church from kindergarten on, and for quietly handling issues that you knew we kids couldn't yet handle. You were, and still are, the perfect mom!

My dad—who taught us there are hard-working people of good character and there are those who are the opposite; the difference has nothing to do with what a person looks like. Second tip: Common sense, don't spend more than you make. Miss you.

Mike—who, since I was so busy writing, jokingly thought I started writing just so I wouldn't have to spend time with him when he retired. Thanks for your patience.

Our children, MK and AE—for listening to Mom's insights even when you would rather do something else and for stepping outside your comfort zones, persevering towards your goals. Always be kind and do the right thing over the easy thing.

Michael Grossman—my first professional boss who always promoted striving to improve. During annual job reviews, you would say, "My job is to empower you to always be your best, continually learning. You should be working hard towards earning my job." Thank you for leading by example.

Peter King, principal, and fellow teachers—to me your business plan seemed to run like this: hire good, hard-working people and empower them to do their job; then step back and let the people do their job; and watch those individuals and the school thrive. Thank you for leading me and empowering me to do my job.

All my previous students—wherever you are, you were the inspiration for this book. May you know that I was blessed by your presence every single day. To those of you who thrived at an early age and to those that struggled, I always believed in you and still do, to this day. Whatever path your lives have taken, may you all know that you have within you whatever it takes to be your greatest self, no matter your age, socioeconomic status, etc. Always continue learning, changing what doesn't work, and maintaining what does work as you continue to grow into adulthood. Love, Miss Margaret (aka Mrs. Hackworthy)

Yes, that's right. I am going to thank my kindergarten teacher, Mrs. McDonald—my very first teacher who always provided positive experiences during my first school involvement. First impressions last a lifetime in children!

My teachers at St. Paul of the Cross Elementary School and Maine South High School—for teaching the subjects, never with agendas. Thank you for teaching, through your challenging educational materials and compassionate instruction, the value of hard work and perseverance when projects were difficult.

Mr. Cunningham—for setting an excellent example as principal by fostering positive principal, teacher, and student interaction. Well done.

St. Thomas the Apostle Teachers—for celebrating students when you felt celebrating was needed, for selflessly teaching, for tirelessly planning and hosting field trips, plays, The Stations, and creating unique, memorable seventh and eighth grade years, grad ceremonies, etc. And equally important, thank you for expecting good behavior, as well as expertly preparing students for high school.

Fathers Kotnik and Simon—who enthusiastically taught students about faith and the importance of working hard, making good choices, and my favorite line, "Never marry a bum!"

Steamboat Springs High School teachers, coaches, and the surrounding community—for supporting students and athletes, instilling in them the attitude that they can achieve anything they work hard towards and put their mind to. Your guidance and inspiration set wonderful examples. Thank you!

Everyone at SPS—special thanks to my coach, Michelle Gano, for suggestions, direction, and encouragement.

Nancy Pile—for support and superb editing, as well as the gift of time.

Cutting Edge Studios - sincerest thanks to Joris and his team for their expertise, direction, and speed bringing this book to fruition.

About the Author

Margaret Huber Hackworthy is a former public relations executive, former preschool and elementary school teacher, mom of two very different children, wife, and current Little Toots ski instructor. She holds a Bachelor of Arts degree in Communications and Public Address and a Masters of Arts in Teaching degree with an emphasis in Early Childhood Education. Margaret encourages parents, caregivers, and teachers to always continue learning as it pertains to the care, raising, and teaching of children of all ages. Her motto for parents, caregivers, and educators, "Knowledge is power," is a reminder that the more you know, the better you equip yourself to make the best decisions with regard to the children in your care. She has plans to return to the early childhood education field soon.

Can You Help?

If you enjoyed this book or found its contents valuable, I would love it if you would leave your honest review. Follow the link below or scan the provided qr code. Use your phone's camera screen and hover over the qr code.

Tap the tinyurl link that will appear on your camera's screen. You will be directed to the *Back to Basics...Parenting in a Chaotic World* landing page. Click on the "Get the Book" button where you will be redirected to the book on Amazon. Scroll down to the bottom of the section titled "Customer Reviews." Type your comments in the "Write A Review" module. Thank you in advance. Your time is greatly appreciated.

tinyurl.com/3kdehzpvbtbparentingworldl

Made in the USA
Monee, IL
27 January 2023

26443316R00089